上海政法学院
Shanghai University of Political Science and Law

法律文书写作与推理

张正怡 钱沂青 黄珮琦 范瑞娟 秦 朗 ◎ 编著

上海社会科学院出版社
SHANGHAI ACADEMY OF SOCIAL SCIENCES PRESS

编著者说明

　　一段时间以来，中国涉外法律专业人才相对匮乏，传统法学教育与英语学习难以找到恰当的融合点，法学实践类课程的双语教学面临着较为艰巨的任务。在全球化背景下，针对涉外法治人才的培养，中国高校要求将对学生法律实践能力的培养融入法学知识的传授与终身学习的过程中，要求学生以英语为工作语言，培养分析和解决法律问题的能力，从而帮助学生在学习期间逐步形成以法律的职业视角和思维分析法律问题，并以法律的职业方式处理法律问题的职业习惯。

　　为此，本书以法律推理为核心，以英语为语言工具，法学专业知识和文书写作技巧并重，在吸收英美法律文书写作推理内容优点的基础上融合涉外法律实务技能的培训，同时结合中国学生在法律英语学习中反馈的问题进行设计和编排，旨在通过系统的训练提高法学专业学生的综合素质与交流能力。本书共分为十七个章节，每个章节包含若干知识点与训练思考。本书采用全英语编排，通过层层递进的训练方式，逐步实现提高学生英文法律文书写作与推理能力的目标，可供相关专业院校和培训机构在法律英语教学阶段参考使用。

　　由于编写时间仓促，本书难免存在疏漏之处，欢迎广大读者及时批评指正。

编著者

2024 年 10 月于上海

Contents

Chapter 1 Understanding Law / 1
    Section 1 What Is Law / 1
    Section 2 Legal Rules / 3
    Section 3 Law and Policy / 4
    Section 4 Classification of Law / 6

Chapter 2 Legal System / 9
    Section 1 Legal System in General / 10
    Section 2 Types of Court / 12
    Section 3 Persons and Documents in Court / 16
    Section 4 Legal Latin / 17
    Section 5 A Career in the Law / 19

Chapter 3 Sources of Law / 22
    Section 1 Understanding Sources of Law / 23
    Section 2 Primary and Secondary Sources of Law / 23
    Section 3 Legislation in General / 26
    Section 4 The Hierarchy of Laws in the US / 28
    Section 5 The Hierarchy of Laws in China / 29

Chapter 4 Citation and Research / 32
    Section 1 Developing Information and Research Skills / 32
    Section 2 Citators / 34
    Section 3 How to Find a Case / 36
    Section 4 Overview of the Research Process / 37

Chapter 5　Case Briefs and Analysis　/　39

　　Section 1　Case Briefs in General　/　40

　　Section 2　Case Briefing Process　/　41

　　Section 3　Precedent and Stare Decisis　/　49

　　Section 4　Judicial Opinions　/　51

Chapter 6　Legal Rule Analysis　/　54

　　Section 1　Elements of Rules　/　54

　　Section 2　Developing a Rule from Multiple Sources　/　57

Chapter 7　Common Law Analysis　/　61

　　Section 1　Legal Reasoning Process　/　61

　　Section 2　Identifying and Selecting Issues for Analysis　/　63

　　Section 3　The Method of Common Law Analysis　/　66

　　Section 4　Statutory Analysis　/　69

Chapter 8　Dispute Resolution-Litigation　/　73

　　Section 1　Definition of Litigation　/　73

　　Section 2　General Introduction of Chinese Civil Procedure System　/　75

　　Section 3　The Sources of the Civil Procedure Law　/　82

Chapter 9　Dispute Resolution-Arbitration　/　90

　　Section 1　Definition from Law Dictionaries　/　91

　　Section 2　International Conventions　/　93

　　Section 3　Commentary/Explanation Report　/　95

　　Section 4　Sample Clause on Arbitration　/　97

　　Section 5　Chinese Arbitration Law　/　102

Chapter 10　Dispute Resolution-Mediation　/　106

　　Section 1　Definition of Mediation　/　106

　　Section 2　International Convention　/　107

　　Section 3　Commentary/ Explanation Report　/　111

　　Section 4　Sample Clauses on Mediation　/　111

　　Section 5　Chinese Mediation Law　/　114

Chapter 11 Writing Basics / 116
   Section 1 Writing Process / 116
   Section 2 Clear Writing and Editing / 119
   Section 3 Punctuation / 129

Chapter 12 Legal Writing in General / 133
   Section 1 Organization / 133
   Section 2 Describe the Law / 136
   Section 3 Explaining the Analysis / 137
   Section 4 Signposting / 138
   Section 5 Drafting the Discussion / 139
   Section 6 IRAC Method / 141
   Section 7 Revising and Editing / 146

Chapter 13 Correspondence / 148
   Section 1 Components of a Letter / 148
   Section 2 Communication Tone / 152
   Section 3 Types of Letters / 156

Chapter 14 Writing in Legal Practice / 161
   Section 1 The Office Memorandum / 161
   Section 2 Brief / 165

Chapter 15 Contract Drafting in General / 173
   Section 1 Overview of a Good Contract / 173
   Section 2 Draft Skills / 174
   Section 3 Preparation Before Drafting a Contract / 175
   Section 4 Structure and Common Types of Contracts / 177

Chapter 16 General Contract Clauses / 180
   Section 1 Cover / 180
   Section 2 Commencement, Whereas and Transition / 181
   Section 3 Definition, Interpretation and Validity / 183
   Section 4 Assignment, Indemnification and Warranty / 185

    Section 5   Rescission and Termination Clause   /   187
    Section 6   Default Clauses   /   188
    Section 7   Dispute Settlement Clause   /   189
    Section 8   Force Majeure Clause   /   191
    Section 9   Miscellaneous   /   192

Chapter 17   Special Contract Clauses   /   193
    Section 1   Confidentiality Clause   /   193
    Section 2   Insurance Clause   /   194
    Section 3   Anti-Competition Clause   /   195
    Section 4   Risk and Title Passing Clause   /   196
    Section 5   Standard Terms   /   197

Appendix   Legal Vocabulary   /   199
    Section 1   Common Latin Words   /   199
    Section 2   Common Legal Terms in Case Reading   /   201
    Section 3   Common Terms in Contract Drafting   /   208

References   /   217

Chapter 1
Understanding Law

  关于什么是法律，一直以来都存在着不同的定义。尽管这些定义的具体内容各不相同，但我们可以从中概括一些共同点：法律由调整个人之间以及个人与社会之间关系的可执行规则组成。这一非常广泛的法律定义意味着：(1)要有法律，就必须有既定的规则，如宪法、法规、行政规章等。(2)这些规则必须能够执行，即法律和秩序必须以司法制度的决议为准。(3)规则须确立个人相互交往和参与社会的所允许的行为。

  法律作为一种社会规范，具有维持社会秩序、规范个人行为、保障个人权利等功能，与其他社会规范和政策有所区别。需要明确的是法律不是万能的，法律有其自身的局限性，因而需要其他社会规范进行调整。根据不同的标准，法律可以进行不同的分类，如公法与私法、程序法与实体法等，在不同的分类中各有其对法律描述的侧重点。

  Law is everywhere. As the poet W. H. Auden pointed out, "The law is The Law." This first chapter sets out to introduce some fundamental ideas that will underpin your understanding of law.

Section 1 What Is Law

  Defining law is a difficult philosophical problem. However, law can generally be understood as the rules and policies for guiding or regulating behavior in society.

A. Definition of Law

  Some of the philosophers' answers, reduced to their most basic forms, are: Law is a system of rules laid down by a body or person with the power and authority to make law.

  Law is what legislators, judges, and lawyers do.

Law is a system of rules grounded on fundamental principles of morality.

Law is a tool of oppression used by the ruling class to advance its own interests.

Understanding Law presupposes the ability to find and read the law, obliges us to think about how we conceptualize complex phenomena like "law", in turn helps us to determine how we should make sensible or reasoned choices about what constitute law in any given situation.

Law as a rule of conduct. (by Aristotle)

Law was a form of social control. (by Plato)

Law was the agreement of reason and nature, the distinction between the just and the unjust. (by Cicero)

Law is a rule of civil conduct prescribed by the supreme power in a state, commanding what is right, and prohibiting what is wrong. (by the British jurist Sir William Blackstone)

Law was a set of rules that allowed one to predict how a court would resolve a particular dispute. (by American eminent jurist Oliver Wendell Holmes)

There are still some common features that revealed the essence of law from these different definitions. First, the law is a series of rules related to conduct or behavior. Second, the law is guaranteed by authority with judicial system. Third, the law is to protect individuals and help people to predict others' conduct.

Black's Law Dictionary (The Tenth Edition) defines "law" as:

1. The regime that orders human activities and relations through systematic application of the force of politically organized society, or through social pressure, backed by force, in such a system; the legal system.

2. The aggregate of legislation, judicial precedents, and accepted legal principles; the body of authoritative grounds of judicial and administrative action; the body of rules, standards, and principles that the courts of a particular jurisdiction apply in deciding controversies brought before them.

3. The set of rules or principles dealing with a specific area of legal system.

4. The judicial and administrative process; legal action and proceedings.

5. A statute.

6. Common law.

7. The legal profession.

Richard A. Posner in *The Problem of Jurisprudence* (1990) explains as "It will help to distinguish three senses of the word law: The first is law as distinctive social institution; that is the sense invoked when we ask whether primitive law is really law. The second is law as a collection of the Statute of Frauds, and so on. The third is law as a source of rights, duties, and powers, as in the sentence "The law forbids the murdering heir to inherit".

B. Function of Law

The functions of law are generally listed as:

1. Maintenance of Public Order and Safety.
2. The Protection of Individual Rights and Liberties.
3. The Organization and Control of the Political Sphere.
4. The Regulation of Economic Activity.
5. The Regulation of Human Relationships.
6. The Preservation of a Moral Order.
7. The Regulation of International Relations.

C. Limitations of Law

Law plays an important role. However, it is not omnipotent and has its own limitations.

1. The scope of law is limited. Law is one of the means to adjust social relations. Some social relations, such as friendship and love, often rely on other social norms other than law.

2. The stability of law cannot always adapt to the changing and developing social reality.

3. The enactment and implementation of laws are influenced by human factors. If there are no good legislators and law executor, it is difficult to play the role of law.

4. Law is restricted by external political, economic, cultural and other social factors.

Exercises:

1. *Could you please give a brief definition of law?*
2. *Explain what a law says: There are several ways to refer to what a law says, as: stipulate/provide/specify/state/set forth/determine/lay down/prescribe. Could you please use some of them to make sentences?*

Section 2 Legal Rules

Rules describe what behavior is permissible or impermissible, what procedures must be followed to achieve certain ends, and what happens to those who do not follow them.

A. Introduction

Rules vary considerably in their scope, clarity and precision. Some rules are created by one case at a time, particularly in the common law. Although they may apply to more situations than just the case at hand, they may be so narrowly tailored that they have little application beyond the particular case from which they arose. Some rules are phrased in a broad or general language.

Legal rules differ from other rules because their creation and enforcement require the participation of the government. The police, courts, and other governmental bodies are responsible for ensuring compliance with these rules.

B. Legal Rules and Social Rules

Law is commonly used to regulate aspects of individual and institutional behavior, indeed legislation in particular is sometimes seen as a paradigm form of regulation. However, law is not the only means of regulation.

As one of a number of possible ways of regulation, law also related to other social rules as:

1. Laws tend to perform the important regulatory functions that often could not be performed by other kinds of rule.

2. Law may be particularly important because of its formal character and the specialist sanctions or remedies that are not available to other forms of regulation.

3. The choice of formal or less formal mechanisms employed may well reflect different priorities, or different social values, regarding the behavior in question.

4. The use of law and legal sanctions is also symbolic: it sends out a powerful message about what society does value.

Generally, laws are identifiable by the fact that they take a form which distinguishes them from other social rules and conventions. Their form tells us that they are derived from an "institutional" source that is socially recognized as having the power to create law. Only rules so created can be said to be legally binding upon the individual, or even upon the state.

Exercises:

1. What ought the law to do?
2. What is the major difference between legal rules and social rules?

Section 3   Law and Policy

Policies are the specific underlying values or purpose for legal rules. Policies reflect varying and sometimes inconsistent views about what is socially good.

Legal rules are based on social judgments, and then tend to act as a shorthand way of deciding what is just in a specific factual situation.

Instead simply asking what is right, for example, a court will first apply the relevant legal rules. A citizen who is 18 years old of age or older cannot be denied the right to vote simply because of the person's age. The answer to the question "Can someone vote in the national election? " depends on whether the person is a citizen and is 18 years of age or older.

Because legal rules are often created to achieve socially desirable goals, they do not necessarily reflect the natural order of things. Change in underlying values or policies will often be followed by change in the legal rules.

The evolution of the law regarding gender-based discrimination is illustrative. The 14th Amendment to the United States Constitution, which went into effect in 1868, provides in part that no state shall "deprive any person of life, liberty, or property, without due process of law". In 1872, the Supreme Court of the United States decided that this provision of the Constitution did not prevent Illinois from refusing to license an otherwise qualified woman to practice law in that state.

Here is the general introduction from the case Bradwell v. Illinois, 83 U.S 130 (1872):

> *Myra Bradwell applied for membership in the Illinois State Bar in accordance with a state statute that permitted any adult of good character and with sufficient training to be admitted. Because she was a woman, however, the Illinois State Bar denied her admission, noting that the "strife" of the bar would surely destroy femininity. Bradwell appealed the decision to the United States Supreme Court, arguing that her right to practice law was protected by the Privileges or Immunities Clause of the Fourteenth Amendment.*

Although the court's sex discrimination decisions leave open some important questions about equality, more than a century later, there can be little question that its outlook has undergone a marked change. It is difficult to imagine the court drawing the same conclusion today as it did in 1872, particularly with the increasing number of women enrolling in law schools, practicing law, and judging cases.

This change in the court's attitude, and ultimately in the law, came as a direct result of changing public views about the role of women. This is not to suggest that judicial or even legislative decisions are made only after a poll is taken; the point is rather that public attitudes and values influence the environment in which these decisions are made.

The law, in turn, is a source of social norms and expectations. What the law requires, permits or prohibits often comes to be associated with what is good or right. Just as the Supreme Court's early decisions helped maintain or create patterns of sex discrimination, so more recent opinions can be credited with easing social tensions.

Exercises:

1. Assume you are a legislator voting on the following bills. Would you vote for or against them? State whether you would vote for or against these bills and explain your decisions.

    (1) A bill requiring persons who ride motorcycles to wear protective helmets.

    (2) A bill prohibiting any person from smoking tobacco.

    (3) A bill requiring couples applying for a marriage license to undergo twelve hours of psychological counseling and testing before the license is granted so they can better determine whether marriage is appropriate for them.

2. Are your decisions consistent with one another?

3. Do you think it is important that your decisions are consistent?

Section 4 Classification of Law

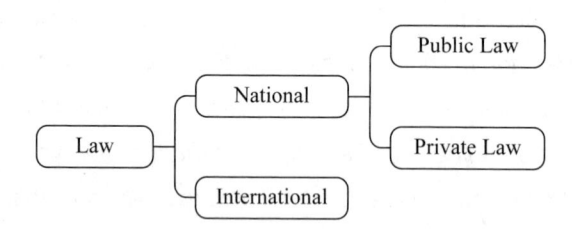

```
                                    ┌── Public Law
                    ┌── National ───┤
        Law ────────┤               └── Private Law
                    └── International
```

A. National Law and International Law

Law can be classified as national (domestic) and international law.

International law can be divided into public international law, which governs relationship between countries, and private international law, which governs which country's law shall apply to individual where there are links with at least two different countries.

B. Public Law and Private Law

National law can also be divided into public law and private (civil) law. Public law involves the State in some way, while private law controls the relationship between individuals. Public law is the body of law addressing individuals and the government, and with the structure and operation of the government itself; it includes constitutional law, criminal law, and administrative law. Private law is the body of law addressing with private persons and their property and relationships. Private law includes contract law, tort law, and company law, etc.

National public law can be divided into: constitutional law, administrative law, and criminal law.

National private law can be divided into many categories, including contract law, tort law, property law, and company law, etc.

C. Substantive Law and Procedural Law

The branches of legal system could also generally be divided into substantive law and procedural law. Substantive law rules rights, obligations, or limitations applicable to people and businesses in a variety of situations. It includes the rights and remedies that are available when one contracting party breached the agreement. Procedural law establishes the rules or the guidelines about how the legal system operates. For example, the length of a statute of limitations for instituting a lawsuit. Procedural law includes criminal procedures law and civil procedures law.

Distinctions between civil and criminal law could be summarized in a simple way as below.

	Civil	**Criminal**
Purpose	Regulation relationships between individuals; Dispute settlement; Enforcement of rights	Prevention of certain types of conduct; Enforcement of behavior; Punishment of offenders
Burden of Proof	Balance of probability	Beyond reasonable doubt
Cases Outcomes	Liability decided civil remedy awarded, e.g. damages; injunction; declaration	Guilt or innocence decided Sentence imposed, e.g. imprisonment community order fine
Terminology	Claimant/Defendant making a claim/ Suing defendant finding a liability	Prosecution/Defendant Charging defendant finding of guilt

However, note that in some areas the distinction between civil and criminal law can be blurred.

Civil law (private law), common law (case law, judge-made law) and criminal law (penal law) are quite different.

The term "civil law" contracts with both "common law" and "private law". In the first sense of the term, civil law refers to a body of law based on written legal codes derived from fundamental normative principles. Legal disputes are settled by reference to this code, which has been arrived at through legislation. Judges are bound by the written law and its provisions.

In contrast, common law was original developed through custom, at a time before laws were written down. Common law is based on precedents created by judicial decisions, which means that the past ruling are taken into consideration when cases are decided. It should be noted that today common law is also codified, i.e. in the written form.

In the second sense of the term, civil law is distinguished from criminal law, and refers to the body of law dealing with non-criminal matters, such as breach of contact.

Exercises:

1. Could you please give definition of civil law, common law and criminal law?

2. Could you please compare civil law and criminal law under Chinese legal system?

Chapter 2
Legal System

　　法系是指具有某种共性或者共同历史传统的法律的总称。尽管法系存在不同的划分和认定，但总体而言，大陆法系与英美法系是影响范围较广的两个法系。大陆法系又被称为民法法系、罗马法系或成文法系。大陆法系是以罗马法为基础发展起来的法律的总称，影响范围主要包括大陆国家及其殖民地。英美法系也称为普通法法系、判例法系、不成文法系、海洋法系等。英美法系以英国中世纪形成的判例法为基础发展而成，影响范围主要包括英国、美国及其殖民地国家或地区。其中，"普通"一词的含义在于法是独立于个人感情和意识之外的客观标准。"不成文"则是强调这些客观标准不是以法条的文字形式表现出来的，而是在法官裁判中确立、在推理中存在。两大法系在法律思维方式、法律渊源、法律分类、诉讼判决及法典编纂等方面存在着差异。

　　在普通法中存在着一个重要的原则，即"遵循先例"，意思是相似的案件应该得到相同的处理。在判决中，如果有成文法依据，法官则先依据成文法规定；如果没有成文法依据，法官应当遵循相同或相似类型的先例。

　　法院体系是法律制度的有机组成部分。英国法院的组织体系根据处理案件类型的不同，主要类别为民事法庭及刑事法庭，各自项下有不同层级的法院负责处理不同的事项。美国联邦体制决定了其法院体系的"双轨制"。各州的法院体系中，最高法院是该州的终审机构，联邦法院的设立和管辖权来自美国宪法的规定。中国法院则分为基层人民法院、中级人民法院、高级人民法院及最高人民法院四级。在法律职业中，律师、检察官和法官是比较常见和比较普遍的职业。在不同国家或不同法律体系下，对法律职业的从事者有不同的从业要求和职责要求。

　　The laws work in a particular jurisdiction. Modern jurists have paid increasing attention to the general concept and minimum requirements of a legal system as distinct from the individual legal norm.

Section 1 Legal System in General

Professor Hart suggested five factors that he believed had to co-exist to create a legal system. These are:

1. Rules that forbid certain conduct and rules that compel certain conduct on pain of sanctions.

2. Rules requiring people to compensate those whom they injure.

3. Rules stating what needs to be done in certain "mechanical" areas of law, such as making a contract or making a will.

4. A system of courts to determine what the rules are, whether they have been broken, and what the appropriate sanction is.

5. A body whose responsibility is to make rules and amend or repeal them when necessary.

As for the categories of legal systems, different textbooks may have different views. Some textbooks listed six categories: civil law, common law, customary law, Muslim law, Talmudic law, and mixed law system, the latter referring not to a single system but to a combination of system. Some textbooks listed five categories: Chinese legal system, Islam legal system, Indian legal system, Common law system and Civil law system.

What we need to focus on are the common law system and civil law system, which have a wider influence.

A. Common Law System v. Civil Law System

Common law system is the system of law developed in England and transferred to most of the English-speaking world. It is based on the case law (common law) formed in the Middle Ages of England, especially after the 11th century and the Norman Conquest. It mainly affected the United Kingdom, the United States, and its colonial countries. The United Kingdom and the United States are the representative countries of the common law system, but there are still internal differences.

Civil law system is the general term of law developed on the basis of Roman law, mainly affecting the countries of continental Europe and its colonial countries. France and Germany are the representative countries of civil law system.

The main differences between the two legal systems.

1. In terms of the characteristics of legal thinking mode, the civil law system belongs to deductive thinking, while the common law system belongs to inductive thinking, focusing on

analogical reasoning.

2. In the terms of source of law, the formal source of law in civil law system is making law, while making law and case law are the official source of law in common law system.

3. In terms of the classification of laws, civil law countries generally regard public law and private law as the basis of legal classification. The basic classification of common law system is common law and equity law.

4. In the aspect of litigation and judgment procedure, civil law system belongs to inquisitorial litigation, while common law system adopts adversarial procedure.

5. In terms of codification, there are representative codes in the major development stages of civil law systems, especially in modern times, large-scale codification activities have been carried out. There was no tendency towards systematic codification of the common law system.

B. Doctrine of Stare Decisis

Stare decisis is a fundamental principle that like cases should be treated alike. The Latin Maxim *stare decisis* (stand by decisions of the past cases) is the basis of the doctrine of precedent.

Precedent, as operated in the English Legal System, requires that in certain circumstances a decision on a legal point made in an earlier case must be followed.

The doctrine is that:

1. All courts are bound to follow decisions made by courts above them in the hierarchy.

2. Appellate courts are normally bound by their own past decision. A past decision is binding only if.

(1) The legal point involved is the same as the legal point in the case now being decided.

(2) The facts of the present case are sufficiently similar to the previous case.

(3) The earlier decision was made by a court above the present court in the hierarchy, or by a court at the same level which is bound by its own past judgements.

(4) The point is argued in the case.

A persuasive precedent is one that the court will consider and may be persuaded by, but which does not have to be followed.

A persuasive precedent comes from a variety of different sources. Decisions by courts outside the English legal system can also have a persuasive effect on English courts.

On the one hand, the precedent brings certainty and predictability of law for the courts and society. The common law settled many legal issues through the precedent and brought stability into many areas of the law. On the other hand, the precedent may take much time to research. There existed some conflicting precedents and in many cases the law can not be found by searching cases. A precedent may be changed or reversed. Since case law is susceptible to change, absolute reliance on it is not possible.

Exercises:

1. *Could you please compare common law system and civil law system from the following aspects to fill the form?*

Compare	Common Law System	Civil Law System
Sources of Law		
Classification of Law		
Codification		
Litigation Proceeding		
Legal Terms		

2. *What is the major difference between binding and persuasive precedent?*
3. *Is there any precedent in Chinese legal system? If it is, please list as one of the examples?*

Section 2　Types of Court

To understand how the common law works, we need to understand English court structure and US court system.

A. Court Structure of the UK

English court system is comprised of a series of courts with different hierarchical levels. The Magistrates' court is at the bottom and the Supreme Court is at the top in the UK. By and large there is fairly clear distinction between courts having civil law and those having criminal law responsibilities.

1. Civil Courts

(1) Supreme Court: Appeals from the Court of Appeal and High Court. Also hears civil appeals from Scotland and Northern Ireland.

(2) Court of Appeal: Appeals from High Court and County Court; Appeal from some tribunals.

(3) High Court:

a. Queen's Bench Division: Common law matters; Commercial Court; Admiralty Court.

b. Family Division: Contested divorce and family proceedings.

c. Chancery Division: Equity, trusts, ect; Companies Court; Patent Court.

d. Administrative Court: Supervisory Jurisdiction over inferior courts and public bodies.

e. Divisional Court: Appeals from the magistrates' courts.

f. Divisional Court: Appeals from the county courts on land and bankruptcy matters.

(4) Magistrates' Court: Family proceeding courts.

(5) Country Courts: Majority of civil litigation, uncontested divorce, and family courts.

2. Criminal Courts

(1) Supreme Court: Appeals from the Court of Appeal and High Court; Appeals from Northern Ireland.

(2) Court of Appeal: Appeal from the Crown Court.

(3) High Court: Queen Bench Division, Case stated by the magistrates' court.

(4) Crown Court: Trials on indictment; Committals for sentence; Appeals from the magistrates' court.

(5) Magistrates' Courts: Trials of summary offences; Committals to the Crown Court.

B. US Court System

Certain basic facts about the American legal system must be recognized.

First of all, statues and precedents (decided cases), in all legal areas, vary from state to state.

Second, each state is free to decide for it questions concerning its common law and interpretation of its own constitutions and statues.

Third, many legal issues arise out of acts or transactions that have contact with more than one state.

1. The Dual System

The trend toward uniform statutes has tended to decrease these conflicts, but many of them still exist. So in studying American Law, students should be aware that different states may have different substantive laws and different choice of law rules regarding a particular legal situation, resulting in the possibility that the choice of forum may affect the substantive rights of parties concerned.

US Judicial Branch also includes court of last resort, intermediate appellate court and trial level courts on both federal and state levels. Here is the general description of federal court system with Supreme Court, Circuit Courts of Appeals and District Courts; state court system with Supreme Court, Appellate Courts and Trial Courts.

A Parallel System of Federal and State Courts

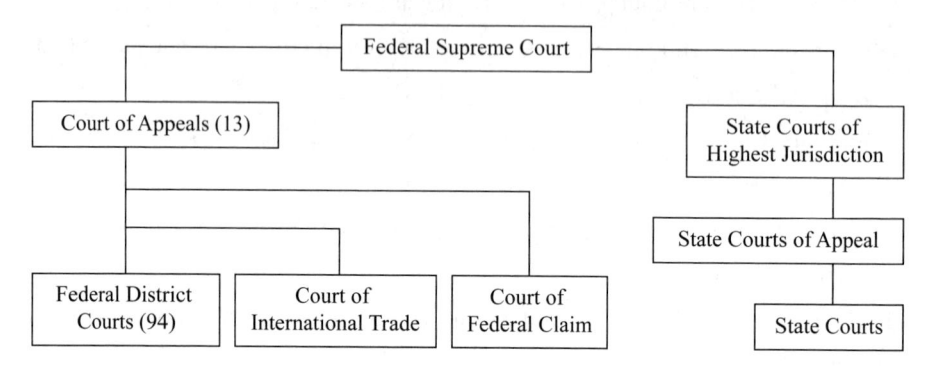

```
                    Federal Supreme Court
           ┌────────────────┴────────────────┐
    Court of Appeals (13)              State Courts of
           │                          Highest Jurisdiction
           │                                 │
           │                          State Courts of Appeal
           │                                 │
  ┌────────┼────────┐                        │
Federal  Court of   Court of             State Courts
District International Federal
Courts(94) Trade    Claim
```

2. Federal Court System

From the 1st Circuit Court to the 13th Circuit Court, Federal Courts are generally defined by geographic boundaries.

Circuit	States Included
1st Circuit	Maine, Massachusetts, New Hampshire, Puerto Rico, Rhode Island
2nd Circuit	Connecticut, New York, Vermont
3rd Circuit	Delaware, New Jersey, Pennsylvania, Virgin Islands
4th Circuit	Maryland, North Carolina, South Carolina, Virginia, West Virginia
5th Circuit	Louisiana, Mississippi, Texas
6th Circuit	Kentucky, Michigan, Ohio, Tennessee
7th Circuit	Illinois, Indiana, Wisconsin
8th Circuit	Arkansas, Iowa, Minnesota, Missouri, Nebraska, North Dakota, South Dakota
9th Circuit	Alaska, Arizona, California, Guam, Hawaii, Idaho, Montana, Northern Mariana Islands, Nevada, Oregon, Washington
10th Circuit	Colorado, Kansas, Oklahoma, Utah, Wyoming
11th Circuit	Alabama, Florida, Georgia
12th Circuit	District of Columbia Circuit
13th Circuit	Federal Circuit

Suppose there would be cases starting from District Court of Florida at the federal court level, the case might proceed to United States Court of Appeals for the 13th Circuit as the middle level appeals court, and might proceed to United Supreme Court as the highest court.

It is the same for state jurisdiction as illustrated by the following chart.

Highest Court	Florida Supreme Court	Indiana Supreme Court
Middle Level Appeals Court	Court of Appeals of Florida	Indiana Court of Appeals
Trial Court	Court for Seminole Country	Marion County Superior Court

District Courts conduct trials about federal matters, such as federal crimes and enforcement of federal statutes. Diversity of citizenship jurisdiction exists when the plaintiff and defendant are from different states or countries. The amount of claimed damages in a diversity of citizenship case must be at least $75,000. Under this circumstance, it is also possible to sue a federal court even though the claim is based on state law.

C. Chinese Court System

There are four tiers of courts in Chines Court System: the Supreme People's Court, the Higher People's Court, the Intermediate People's Court, and the Basic People's Court, as well as special people's courts for military, railway and water transportation.

The Supreme People's Court supervises the administration of justice by the people's courts at various local levels and by the special people's courts. People's courts at higher levels supervise the administration of justice by those at lower levels. The powers of the Supreme People's Court include adjudicating the cases, interpreting judicial decisions, approving death sentences and dealing with the corresponding cases of appeal and protest.

Higher People's Courts are established in provinces, autonomous regions and municipalities directly under the Central Government; Intermediate People's Courts are established by region within provinces, autonomous regions and municipalities directly under the Central Government; and the Basic People's Courts are established in counties, autonomous counties and municipal districts. The people's courts exercise judicial power independently, in accordance with the provisions of the law, and are not subject to interference by any administrative organ, public organization or individual.

Exercises:

1. *Could you please organize and devise a form to show UK civil court system as well as UK criminal court system?*

2. Suppose there would be cases starting from District Court of Delaware at the federal court level, where might the case be judged if it proceeds to some higher level jurisdictions?

Section 3   Persons and Documents in Court

A. Person in Court

Here are some possible definitions for persons in court.

1. judge

public official who has the authority to hear and decide cases

2. claimant

person who initiates a civil lawsuit

3. defendant/respondent

person who is sued in a civil lawsuit

4. expert witness

person who has specialized knowledge of a particular subject who is called to testify in court

5. advocate

person who pleads cases in court

6. appellant

person who appeals a decision to a higher court

7. clerk

employee who takes records, files papers and issues processes

8. bailiff

officer of the court whose duties include keeping order and assisting the judge and jurors

9. reasonably prudent person

hypothetical person who uses good judgment or common sense in handling practical matters; such a person's actions are the guide in determining whether an individual's actions were reasonable

B. Documents in Court

Here are some possible definitions for documents in court.

1. affidavit

a writ statement that somebody makes after they have sworn officially to tell the truth, which might be used as proof in court

2. answer

the principal pleading by the defendant in response to a complaint

3. brief

a document or set of documents containing details about a court case

4. complaint

in civil law, the first pleading filed on behalf of a plaintiff, which initiates a lawsuit, setting forth the facts on which the claim is based

5. injunction

an official order from a court to obtain an order, ruling or decision

6. motion

an application to a court to obtain an order, ruling or decision

7. notice

a document providing notification of a fact, claim or proceeding

8. pleading

a formal written statement setting forth the cause of action or the defense in a case

9. writ

a document informing someone that they will be involved in a legal process and instructing them what they must do

Exercises:

Please match each verb used by the lawyer with its definition: draft/issue/file (with)/serve (on someone)/submit

1. *to deliver a legal document to someone, demanding that they go to a court of law or that they obey an order*
2. *to produce a piece of writing or a plan that you intend to change later*
3. *to deliver a document formally for a decision to be mad by others*
4. *to officially record something, especially in a court of law*
5. *to produce something official*

Section 4　Legal Latin

Lawyers use Latin words and expressions when writing legal texts from statutes to email. Here are Latin words or expressions with English equivalent or the explanation of use.

More Latin words are listed in the Appendix.

1. ad hoc

for this purpose (often used as adjective before a noun)

2. et alii (et al.)

and others (usually used to shorten a list of people, often a list of authors, appellants or defendants)

3. et cetera (etc.)

and other things of the same kind (used to shorten a list similar items)

4. exempli gratia (e.g.)

for example (used before one or more examples are given)

5. id est (i. e.)

that is (used to signal an explanation or paraphrase of a word preceding it)

6. per se

by itself (often used after a noun to indicate the thing itself)

7. sic

thus (used after a word to indicate the original, usually incorrect, spelling or grammar in a text)

8. versus (vs. or v.)

against (abbreviate to "v." in case citations, but to "vs." in all other instances)

9. de facto

in fact

10. ipso facto

by that very fact itself

11. inter alia

among other things

12. per annum

per year

13. pro forma

as a matter of form

14. pro rata

proportionally

15. quorum

number of shareholders or directors who have to be present at a board meeting so that it can be validly conducted

16. sui juris

of one's own right; able to exercise one's own legal rights

17. ultra vires

beyond the legal powers of a person or a body

18. videlicet (viz)

as follows

Exercise:

Please underline the common Latin words and phrases in the excerpt. Do you know what they mean?

The claims for breach of contract fails inter alia to state facts sufficient to constitute a cause of action, is uncertain as to what contract plaintiffs are suing on, and is uncertain in that it cannot be determined whether the contract sued on is written, oral or implied by conduct.

The complaint alleges breach of contract as follows: "At all times herein mentioned, plaintiffs were a part sic to the Construction Contract as well as intended beneficiaries to each sub-contract for the construction of the house. In light of the facts set out above, defendants, and each of them, have breached the Construction contract."

On its face, the claim alleges only that defendants "breach the Construction Contract". But LongCo is not a party to the Construction Contract. Therefore, LongCo cannot be liable for its breach.

Section 5　A Career in the Law

A. Legal Profession

1. Lawyers

(1) advocate

general term used in Scottish law for someone whose job is to give advice to people about the law and speak for them in court

(2) attorney

mostly US term for someone whose job is to give advice to people about the law and speak for them in court

(3) barrister

mostly UK/Australian/Canadian term, more specific term for someone who is qualified to give specialist legal advice and can argue a case in both higher and lower courts

(4) lawyer

mostly US term used in Scottish law for someone whose job is to give advice to people about the law and speak for them in court

(5) solicitor

mostly UK/Australian/Canadian term, more specific term for someone who is trained to prepare cases and give advice on legal subjects and can represent people in lower courts

2. Prosecutor

The prosecutors in different countries play different roles which depends on the judicial system. In general, the prosecutor usually represents the state against crime. In China, prosecutors conduct legal supervision according to law, prosecute on behalf of the State and investigate certain criminal cases directly. Prosecutors in the United States contain the assistant attorney general, prosecutors, federal and local prosecutors and support staff. In general, prosecutors must be the members of the state lawyers association. An independent counsel is an official who is responsible for investigating and prosecuting criminal acts committed by senior state officials. It is the special system in the US.

3. Judges

Article III of the US Constitution governs the appointment, tenure, and payment of Supreme Court justices, and federal circuit and district judges. These judges, often referred to as "Article III judges", are nominated by the president and confirmed by the US Senate. These judges hold their office during good behavior, which means they have a lifetime appointment, except under very limited circumstances. They can be removed from office only through impeachment by the House of Representatives and conviction by the Senate. Article III judgeships are created by legislation enacted by Congress. Article I judges do not have a life tenure or protections from salary decrease as do Article III court judges have.

B. Legal Education

In English-speaking countries, the bar is a term for the legal profession itself, while a bar association is the association which regulates the profession. A person who qualifies to practice law is admitted to the bar; in the US, a law-school graduate must pass the bar examination. Education of a lawyer might undergo the following steps:

1. Prerequisites for studying law
2. Main students covered at law school

3. Bar examination
4. Student clerkship

C. Law-firm Structure

Senior Partners, Full Partners, Salaried Partner

Salaried Lawyer

Associate

Paralegal

Exercise:

Please describe a law firm using the following phrases:

is/are headed/assisted /managed by

is/are responsible for/in charge of

report to

Chapter 3
Sources of Law

本章主要介绍法律渊源与不同层级的法律效力。法律渊源，是指法的效力来源，具体指法获得成立的方式和各种表现形式。法的渊源又可分为正式渊源和非正式渊源。制定法是法律的正式渊源之一，不同国家机关根据具体职权和程序制定的各种规范性文件是直接作为法官审理案件之依据的规范来源，如宪法、法律、法规等，主要为制定法。非正式渊源并未在正式法律中得到权威性的明文体现，但作为具有法律意义的准则和观念也可能影响到案件的结果。

英美法系与大陆法系在法律渊源方面存在显著差异，英美法系中的判例法作为法律渊源的表现形式之一，在司法案件的审判实践中发挥着重要的作用。对该法系中不同的法律渊源进行分类，可以更加清晰地明确其对案件的实际参考作用。大陆法系中，立法是开启制定法的首要环节，包括法律的起草、引入、通过以及最后的生效等过程。

法律的效力层级是在一个国家的法律体系中，不同形式的法律效力是否相同，如果不同，它们之间的效力级别如何排序。本章以美国、中国为例，分别介绍其各自法律渊源的位阶。前者主要包括宪法、法规、行政规定及司法判例，后者主要包括宪法、法律、行政法规、部门规章、地方性规章、地方性法规、自治条例、单行条例等。法律位阶是一个相对概念，通过比较不同的规范性文件，效力等级高的作为上位法，效力等级低的作为下位法，这样解决了它们之间的冲突。

The law library contains all kinds of sources you need to consult when you research a legal question. By the end of your legal research class, you will be familiar with many sources of law.

Section 1　Understanding Sources of Law

Sources of law in Roman law is called Fontes Juris, later in German Rechtsquellen. Sources of law may be understood as a point of origin for law or legal analysis; or something that provides authority for legislation and for judicial decisions.

Sources of law could be referred as:

1. The origins of legal concepts and ideas.
2. Governmental institutions that formulate legal rules.
3. The published manifestations of the laws.

We could also ask:

1. Where could we find the laws?
2. Where does the judge obtain the rules by which to decide cases?

Authority is official right or permission to act, while Legal Authority is a source cited in support of a legal argument.

The formal sources of law can be broadly categorized into the main types of statutory law, case law, customary law, doctrine, and jurisprudence.

1. The statutory law refers to the normative documents formulated and promulgated by state organs in accordance with certain procedures and usually expressed in the form of articles.
2. Case law refers to the law based on decisions made by judges in earlier cases.
3. Customary law refers to customs and practices that have been recognized in a certain way by a competent state authority and are given the effect of legal norms.
4. A doctrine is a jurist's opinion or viewpoint on a legal issue.
5. Jurisprudence usually refers to the basic spirit of the law.

Exercises:

1. *How do you understand sources of law?*
2. *Could you please give an example as sources of law?*

Section 2　Primary and Secondary Sources of Law

Primary sources and secondary sources are all sources of law, but they are used in different ways. Their use depends on the information they contain and how authoritative they are. Primary sources contain the law itself and may be mandatory authority. Secondary sources contain commentary on the law.

The Constitution of the United States is the supreme law of the land. It is only one of many sources of American law. In addition to the Constitution, American law comprises common law, statutes, and administrative rules and regulations. Here is the general classification of primary and secondary sources in the U.S.

Authority	Primary or Secondary	Mandatory	Persuasive
US Constitution	Primary	Always mandatory	
US Supreme Court Case	Primary	Always mandatory	
US Circuit Court Case	Primary	Mandatory to circuit court itself and to federal district courts within deciding circuit	Very persuasive outside of deciding circuit
US District Court Case	Primary	Mandatory only to deciding court	Very persuasive within circuit, somewhat persuasive to others
US Statute	Primary	Mandatory, preempts conflicting state statutes	
US Regulation	Primary	Mandatory if within the scope of enabling statute	
State Constitution	Primary	Mandatory in state	Persuasive in other states
State Supreme Court Case	Primary	Mandatory in state and to federal district court sitting in diversity in that state	Reasonably persuasive in other states
State appellate and trial court cases	Primary	Mandatory only within appropriate state subdivision	Reasonably persuasive in comparable subdivisions
Restatements of law	Secondary		Highly persuasive, often more than persuasive case law
Treatises	Secondary		Can be very persuasive
Law review articles	Secondary		Can be quite persuasive, depending on author and topic match
Legal encyclopedias etc.	Secondary		Very little persuasive value

Exercises:

Your client is Sarah Berg, who owns an apartment complex. As part of a remodeling project, she hired a paint contractor, Deco, Inc. to strip the paint off the walls of the common areas in the apartment building and repaint them. Several of the tenants became ill after inhaling fumes from the paint remover. They have brought suit against Berg and Deco in state court, alleging that the workers were negligent in using the paint remover without adequate ventilation and without warning the tenants that they should vacate the premises during the paint removal process. Berg has an insurance policy that excludes from coverage damages or injuries resulting from "dispersal, release, or escape of pollutants". The insurer has denied coverage on the grounds that the pollution exclusion clause applied to indoor release of pollutants. Thus, the resulting injuries are excluded from coverage. In researching the issue of insurance coverage, you have found the following:

(1) A law review article discussing whether the standard pollution exclusion clause in an insurance policy applied to indoor releases of contaminants.

(2) An opinion by the highest court of another state addressing the same issue in a case with similar facts (insecticide sprayed inside an apartment building).

(3) An opinion by a federal court of appeals addressing the same issue in a case within similar facts (fumes from house paint) and applying the law of another state when that state's courts had not decided this specific issue.

(4) An opinion by a federal district court addressing the same issue in a case with similar facts (fumes from diesel fuel sprayed inside the foundation of an apartment building to eradicate termites) and applying the law of your state when your state's courts have not addressed this specific issue.

(5) An article in a national legal periodical on the history of the pollution exclusion clause.

(6) An opinion concerning an automobile liability policy, decided by the highest court of your state, in which the court set out certain principles regarding the construction of insurance policies.

(7) An opinion by a federal court of appeals addressing the same issue in a case with similar facts (carbon monoxide released by a faulty furance) and applying the law of another state, replying on a desicion by an intermediate level court in that state.

(8) An opinion by the same court described in deciding the same issue but reaching the opposite conclusion based on decisions by the highest court in still another state.

Please divide these sources into three categories.

(1) primary authority that is binding

(2) primary authority that is persuasive

(3) secondary authority

Section 3 Legislation in General

Pressure for new laws comes from a variety of sources, such as government policy, reports, pressure groups, etc. The growth in legislation has been a key feature in modern legal system. It reflects the extent to which social life has become more complex, and the government has extended its control over our activities, both in the areas of business and commerce, and in the social sphere, where many important fields, such as employment, child case, and social security law, owe their modern existence almost exclusively to statue.

A statue law is a document which contains laws made by the Parliament. Statute law is also referred to as Act of Parliament. Statute law is now found virtually all fields of law and govern all sorts of activities.

Statute law enjoys several advantages over case law:

1. There is the opportunity for consultation.

2. Law can be passed to avoid future problems.

3. The change to the law is usually prospective, thus not affecting existing contracts, etc..

4. The law is known in advance, rather than after the judgment in a case.

5. An act can cover a wide range of points.

6. Statutory law supersedes common law.

7. It cannot normally be challenged because of the sovereignty of the Parliament.

The government usually sets out its legislative program for the parliamentary session. Taking the UK as an example, there are several processes for making laws.

A. The Drafting Process

1. A draft act is called a bill.

2. The vast majority of bills are introduced by the government of the day.

These government bills are drafted by the parliamentary counsel to the Treasury.

3. The government department responsible for the legislation will give detailed instructions to the parliamentary counsel.

4. Main criticisms to the quality of draftsmanship are: the language used in statutes was obscure and complex; over-elaboration in an effort to obtain certainty; illogical and unhelpful structure; amendment of previous Acts by later Acts making it difficult to discover the current law.

5. The government can say that no written statement compatible with European Convention on human rights could be made but that it wishes to proceed with the Bill.

B. Introducing a Bill

Each bill goes through a number of states before it becomes an Act. If the bill is voted against at the Second Reading or the Third Reading in either House, then it does not become law.

1. Bills can be introduced into the Parliament in the House of Commons or the House of Lords.

2. Government bills are introduced by the government through the relevant minister; such bills are known as Government Bills and will almost always become law as the government usually has a majority in the House of Commons.

C. Passing a Bill

A bill may be introduced in either the House of Commons or the House of Lords, but it has to go through the same procedure in each House and pass all states of the legislative process in order to become law.

1. First Reading—a formality at which the title of the bill read out and a day named for the Second Reading.

2. Second Reading—the main debate on the principles of the bill.

3. Committee Stage—a consideration of each clause of the bill.

4. Report Stage—a report to the whole House of amendments proposed by the Committee stage.

5. Third Reading—the final vote on the bill; there will be a further debate about the bill only if at least six members request it.

6. The Other House—if the bill stated in the House of Commons, then the above five stages are carried out in the House of Lords, and vice versa.

7. Royal Assent—a formal assent to the bill by the Monarch. The bill is now an Act of Parliament.

D. Coming into Force

An Act of Parliament comes into force on the commencement date given in the Act; or the date set by the appropriate Government Minister if there is an "appointed day" section;

or midnight following the Royal Assent if there is no indication in the Act.

Exercises:

1. *Could you please briefly describe the legislation process in the US?*
2. *Could you please describe and explain the legislation process in China?*

Section 4   The Hierarchy of Laws in the US

For internal laws of the US, four basic kinds of laws exist: constitutions, statutes or ordinances, administrative regulations and judge-made law.

These sources form a hierarchy with constitution at the top and judge making laws at the bottom.

A. Constitution

Constitution includes the US Constitution as well as state constitutions. With a jurisdiction, the constitution is the highest authority; statutes, regulations, and common law must not conflict with the constitution. Within a jurisdiction, the constitution is the highest authority; statutes, regulations and common law must not conflict with the constitution. Constitution provides that the Constitution and federal laws pursuant to the Constitution "shall be the supreme law of the land".

B. Statues

Statutes create categorical rules to address particular problems. The Food, Drug and Cosmetic Act, for example, was adopted by the Congress to ensure the safety and healthfulness of the nation's food supply. A statute is controlling as to the subject it encompasses, unless the statute is unconstitutional.

C. Regulations

The federal government and most states have many agencies with diverse responsibilities. Regulations are rules promulgated by such agencies to help implement specific statutes. For example, the "laws" relating to declarations of nutritional information required on the packages of certain foods are largely administrative regulations promulgated by the Food and Drug Administrative regulations have the same legal effect as statutes, so long as they are consistent with the Constitution and relevant statutes.

D. Case Laws

Case Laws often interpret or apply constitutions, statutes or regulations. At other times, when such law is not applicable, they interpret or apply a body of judge-made law known as common law. In either situation, law is made whenever a court decides a case. Once a constitutional provision, statute, or regulation has been construed by a court, that construction becomes law.

Exercises:

1. How do you understand the "Supremacy Clause" in the US?
2. Based on sources of law on the federal level of the US, could you please list sources of law on the state level of the US?

Section 5   The Hierarchy of Laws in China

The following chart may describe current hierarchy of law from the domestic law area in China.

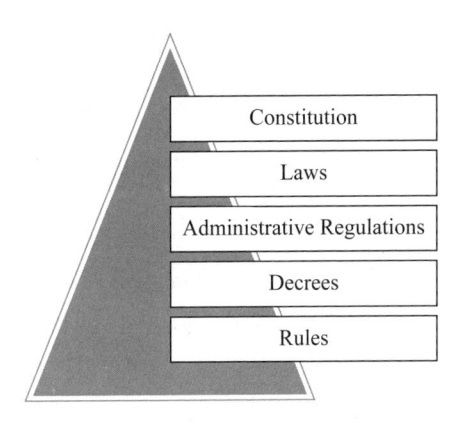

```
Constitution
Laws
Administrative Regulations
Decrees
Rules
```

A. Constitution

The Constitution is the fundamental law of the country and the main source of socialist law in China. The contents are stipulated in the Constitution, the procedures for its formulation and amendment, and the validity of the Constitution is different from other laws and regulations.

The Constitution has the supreme force of law, all laws, administrative regulations and local regulations shall not contradict the Constitution.

B. Laws

They can be divided into two categories: one is the basic laws which are enacted and amended by the National People's Congress.

Civil Code of the People's Republic of China
Adopted at the 3rd Session of the Thirteenth National People's Congress of the People's Republic of China on May 28, 2020

The other is the laws which are enacted and amended by the Standing Committee of National People's Congress.

Trademark Law of the People's Republic of China
Adopted at the 24th Session of the Standing Committee of the Fifth National People's Congress on August 23, 1982

C. Administrative Regulations

Administrative Regulations refer to the normative documents on state administration and management activities made by the State Council, the highest administrative organ of the state, in accordance with and for the implementation of the Constitution and laws.

Implementing Regulations of the Trademark Law of the People's Republic of China
Promulgated by the State Council on August 3, 2002

D. Decrees

Decrees refer to local decrees, autonomous decrees and special decrees. Article 63 of Law on Legislation of the People's Republic of China provides: In light of the specific situations and actual needs of the jurisdiction, the People's Congress of a province, autonomous region, municipality directly under the central government and the Standing Committee thereof may enact local decrees provided that they shall not contravene any provision of the Constitution, national law and administrative regulations.

E. Rules

Rules refer to administrative and local rules.

Article 71 of Law on Legislation of the People's Republic of China provides: The various ministries, commissions, the People's Bank of China, the Auditing Agency, and a body directly under the State Council exercising regulatory function, may enact administrative rules within the scope of its authority in accordance with national law, administrative regulations, as well as decisions and orders of the State Council.

A matter on which an administrative rule is enacted shall be a matter which is within the scope of implementing national law, administrative regulations, and decisions or orders issued by the State Council. Article 73, Paragraph 1 provides: The People's Government of a province, autonomous region, municipality directly under the central government or a major city may enact local rules in accordance with national law, administrative regulations and local decrees of the province, autonomous region, or municipality directly under the central government.

Exercises:

1. Please discuss the following documents: Whether they would be regarded as sources of law in China?

    (1) Judicial Interpretations

    (2) Case Laws(Precedents)

    (3) Jurisprudence

2. Please read the following text, and judge which type of sources of law they are.

    (1) Citizens of the People's Republic of China have the duty as well as the right to receive education. The state promotes the all-round moral, intellectual and physical development of children and young people.

    (2) Anyone who commits a crime shall be equal in applying the law. No one is privileged to be beyond the law.

    (3) A shareholder may not withdraw its capital contribution after registration of the company.

    (4) PRC Regulations for the Administration of Foreign-invested Banks, which has established the criteria for setting up branches are lowered for foreign banks.

    (5) This Convention does not apply to the liability of the seller for death or personal injury caused by the goods to any person.

Chapter 4
Citation and Research

除了与法律相关的技能之外，法律工作者也应当注重培养自己的信息素养和涉及多重领域知识的研究技能，以及实用的 IT、沟通技能等。

法律检索能力，是法律人必须掌握的且最基本的实务技能之一。判例法国家一般将他们的法院判决收辑成为案例汇编。案例汇编有两种：官方案例汇编和非官方案例汇编。目前，非官方案例汇编被政府、法院和律师界广泛采用。美国司法案例汇编的检索主要通过两个途径，其一是 Lexis Nexis 的谢泼德引证（Shepard's Citations）方法，该方法将所有公开发表的法律数据收集起来并做好索引；其二是汤森路透出版公司（Thomson Reuters Westlaw）提供的关键引用（KeyCite）检索服务方式，它整合了所有在线的判例法和成文法，可以自动通知读者相关案例、法律条文、行政裁决和规章的变化，包括提供曾引用某一案件的其他各案件、行政判解、某一案件直接上诉的历史等。

How do we find the law on a particular issue? That is a question of developing the appropriate research skills to do the job. Research skills matter, particularly for new lawyers, not just at university or college, but when working in a wide range of trainee and paralegal roles.

Section 1 Developing Information and Research Skills

Developing your own information literacy and research skills involves a mix of domain knowledge, plus functional IT, research, and communication skills.

A. Domain Knowledge: Knowledge of and about law

There are generic types of knowledge that one should possess in order to have a full appreciation of the legal system in general, to understand how disputes might be resolved, to understand and apply various legal principles and standards, and to appreciate the context in which a legal problem or dispute arises. Some of the types of knowledge that are the most useful, and that would most pervasively affect one's ability to derive the maximum benefit from legal education. These types include: a broad understanding of history, a basic understanding of political thought and theory, knowledge about economics, financial and social interaction.

B. Media Literacy: Produce Content across a Range of Media

A law student should be able to understand and use the media properly, be able to think and produce information in the process of education, and be able to interpret media messages from a critical perspective.

C. Learning Skills: Ability to Learn in a Technology-rich Environment

Much of the work done by law students and lawyers involves the careful reading and complex understanding of judicial opinions, statutes, documents, and other written materials. The study and practice of law require the ability to read and assimilate large amounts of material, often in very short periods of time. In a technology-rich environment, rigorous engagement in the careful reading and understanding and critical analysis of large volumes of complex written materials places greater demands on the skills of learning.

D. Information Management: Safely Store, Manage, and Share Information

The study and practice of law require the ability to organize large amounts of information, to identify objectives, and to create a structure for applying that information in an efficient way in order to achieve desired results.

E. Information Literacy: Find, Interpret and Evaluate Information

A person should have participated in a program that required extensive library research and analysis of the vast amount of information obtained from that research before entering a law school, or he would be at a serious disadvantage. A legal education should plan courses and experiences in research strategies, conducting extensive library research, and analyzing, organizing, and presenting large amounts of material. Word processing or computerized legal research is also increasingly important.

Exercises:

1. *Please explain key skills in legal research.*
2. *How to expand domain knowledge through information management?*

Diagram

- **Information and Research Skills** (center)
  - Domain Knowledge: Knowledge of and about law
  - Learing Skills: Ability to learn in a technology-rich environment
  - Information Literacy: Find, interpret and evaluate information
  - Information Management: Safely store, manage and share information
  - Media Literacy: Produce content across a range of media

Section 2 Citators

Although citators are one of the last sources in a legal research class, they are one of the most important tools in legal research. Citators are important because they allow the legal researcher to ascertain the history of a case and which cases and other legal sources have cited to the case.

A set of books or database that lists relevant legal events subsequent to a given case, statute or other authority. Two leading citators are Shepard's Citations and KeyCite in the US. Without correctly using a citator, one may fail to ascertain that a case upon which he or she is relying has been reversed or overruled. The citator has two primary use. It is used to determine the current status of a case, whether the case is still authoritative. The citatory is also used as a case-finding tool.

A. Shepard's Citations

The researcher uses the citator to verify the status of a case and update it. Frank Shepard founded Shepard's Citations Company in 1873 in Illinois, and the company published citators for many years. Shepard's Citations is now a part of LexisNexis, which continue to publish a separate set of citators for each jurisdiction.

There are several steps in Shepardizing Procedure:

1. Locate the correct set of Shepard's Citations and be ready to record results.

Look at the Shepardizing information for DePierre v. United States. DePierre was decided on June 9, 2011. The case is published in United States Supreme Court Reports, Lawyer's Edition, beginning on page 114 of volume 180 and Supreme Court Reporter, beginning on page 2,225 of volume 131, within a few weeks of the case being decided. Thus, DePierre could be Shepardized using the citation from Supreme Court Reporter or United States Supreme Court Reports, Lawyer's Edition.

2. Determine which Shepard's Citations volume to use.

The next step is to determine which volume of the ones listed on the front cover you will need to use. The hardbound volumes need not be consulted because they date from before 2011, and DePierre was decided in 2011. Because the case is so recent, changes are the last issue or issues are the only issues of Shepard's Citation to contain information on DePierre.

3. Check each Shepard's Citations volume identified.

It is important that you check each of the volumes you have identified because they are not cumulative. This means that each of the Shepard's Citations volumes listed on the front of the latest Shepard's Citation issue contains different information from any other volume.

B. KeyCite

KeyCite is the online citator introduced into Westlaw a number of years ago and became the exclusive citator on Westlaw in June 1999.

Keycite is used to determine if a case is still authoritative, and it is used to find other cases that are cited to the case you are cite-checking. When viewing cases in Westlaw, it is good practice to check the upper left-hand corner of the screen for case status flag (a red triangular warning flag or a yellow triangular warning flag), a blue uppercase "H" symbol and a green uppercase "C" symbol.

Exercises:

1. *The homepage of Shepard's Citations is located at http://www.lexisnexis.com/ shepards and features a number of online brochures. Review several of the brochures.*
2. *Please try to use Westlaw Database and explain how to check citations using KeyCite.*

Section 3 How to Find a Case

A case is generally consists of:

1. Case name
2. Court rendering the opinion
3. Citation
4. Justice who wrote the opinion
5. Opinion(stating the issue raised, describing the parties and facts, discussing the relevant law, and rendering judgment)
6. Votes of the court

Citation formats exist for many different types of legal sources, including cases, statutes and secondary legal materials. Understanding the basic format for each of these different types of sources will enable the researcher to more independently locate materials in the law library.

Citation is made up of :

1. Names of parties involved in the lawsuit
2. The volume number of the reporter containing the full text of the case
3. The abbreviated name of that case reporter
4. The page on which the case begins
5. The year the case was decided
6. The name of the court deciding the case

A format could be inferred as:

Plaintiff v. Defendant

Vol. Collection Starting Page (court-deciding year)

For example: Marbury v. Madison, 5 U.S. 137 (1803)

Here is part of abbreviation for title.

A.	Atlantic Reporter
Cal.	California Reporter
F.	Federal Reporter
F. 2d	Federal Reporter, 2nd Series

(To be Continued)

F. 3d	Federal Reporter, 3rd Series
F. Supp.	Federal Supplement
L. Ed.	Lawyers' Edition
P.	Pacific Reporter
S.Ct.	Supreme Court Reporter
U.S.	United States Reports

Exercise:

Please explain the following citations.

(1) Hebb v. Severson, 201 P. 2d 156(Wash.1948)

(2) Morgan v. United States, 298 U.S. 468, 56 S.Ct 906, 80L.Ed.1288 (1936)

(3) Roe v. Wade, 410 U.S. 113, 93 S.Ct.705, 35 L.Ed.2d.147(1973)

Section 4 Overview of the Research Process

Generally, legal research encompasses a series of steps, beginning with a research problem and ending with an answer to the problem. Several steps of legal research could be followed.

1. Gather all relevant factual information.

2. Identify relevant key words that you will use as search terms in indexes to secondary and primary sources.

3. Use secondary sources.

4. Find relevant primary sources.

5. Update primary sources.

6. Determine whether you have complete the research.

7. Formulate an answer to the research problem.

Here are some Chinese legal databases.

Ministry of Justice of the People's Republic of China	http://www.chinalaw.gov.cn/(Chinese Version) http://en.moj.gov.cn/ (English Version)
PKU Law	http://www.pkulaw.cn/(Chinese Version) https://www.pkulaw.com/english/(English Version)
China Judgements Online	http://wenshu.court.gov.cn/
The Supreme People's Court of the People's Republic of China	https://www.court.gov.cn/ (Chinese Version) https://english.court.gov.cn/ (English Version)

Exercises:

1. *Internet Research exercises:*

    http://www.lawschool.cornell.edu

    http://www.versuslaw.com

    http://www.findlaw.com

    http://www.washlaw.edu

    http://www.americanbar.org

    http://www.law.com

2. *Please search cases in particular areas through China Judgments Online.*

Chapter 5
Case Briefs and Analysis

制作案例摘要是阅读案例时十分重要的环节。案例摘要既需要简洁明了，以方便快速查阅和回答他人的提问，又要全面涵盖案例要点内容，避免出现疏漏。虽然案例摘要的形式和侧重点有所不同，但基本都须涵盖案件事实、争议焦点、相关法律法规、法院裁决及理由、相关政策等要点。案例摘要能帮助读者在复杂的案例中把握主线，节省归纳时间，方便后续分析。

Courts in our society decide what the law means and how it should be applied to a specific situation. Courts sometimes interpret rules that are codified in statutes, regulations or constitutions. At other times they make their own rules as they decide cases, forming the common law.

Although the following parts may sometimes appear in a different order, common law cases generally follow the following structure and order:

1. Discussion of the procedural posture of the case
2. Summary of the facts
3. Legal issues before the court and sometimes followed by the legal theories of the disputing parties
4. Court's decision or the holding of the case
5. Court's reasoning
6. Relevant rules from the decision
7. Other procedural decision
8. Other court opinions such as concurring opinion or dissenting opinion

Section 1　Case Briefs in General

A case brief is a written summary of your analysis of a case that should help you prepare for class or writing an assignment. Case briefs are not to be confused with trial and appellate court briefs, which are written to persuade a court to adopt your client's position. Many formats exist for case briefing, but they all include the elements described here.

A description of the facts
A statement of the legal issue or issues presented for decision
The relevant rule or rules of law
The holding
The disposition
Policies and reasons that support the holding

Exercise: Read the following brief, and illustrate some components.

State v. Jones (1991)

Jones appeals his conviction for possession of marijuana. When the police stopped and searched Jones's van, they found an ounce of marijuana in a backpack in the far near of the vehicle. Although Jones admitted he knew the marijuana was there, he defended against the charge by claiming that the backpack and drugs belonged to a hitchhiker who had been riding with him and who had accidentally left them in the van. In this state, it is presumed that drugs are in the possession of the person who controls them. The issue in this case is whether the marijuana was within Jones's control even though it was in backpack in the rear of his van. That the backpack and drugs may have been owned by someone else is irrelevant. Public policy dictates that possession should not be synonymous with ownership because the difficulty of proving ownership would permit too many drug offenders to evade prosecution. It is sensible to assume that anything inside a vehicle is within the control of the driver. We hold that Jones possessed marijuana because the backpack was within Jones's van and thus under his control. Affirmed.

Exercises:

1. *What are the main elements for a case brief?*

2. Understand the legal issue in your own words.

Section 2   Case Briefing Process

Each component of a case will be discussed separately with an emphasis on identifying and understanding that component. Because of the weblike nature of a judicial opinion, no method will result in instant identification or understanding of the components. As you gain experiences at briefing case, you will develop a format that suits your particular abilities and needs. The following method should prove helpful as a starting point and framework for your analysis.

A. Read the Opinion Carefully

During your initial reading you will gain a general understanding of who the parties were, how the dispute originated, and what effect the court's decision had on the parties. You will also form tentative theories concerning the basic components of the opinion that you will test and clarify during your later reading. After you have acquired a basic understanding of the facts of the case and the "real world" implications of the court's decision, you can figure out what the court decided.

B. Identify the Holding

The holing is the actual decision in the case. It is the answer to the legal question presented to the court. Identifying the holding requires you to study the opinion and determine what the court actually decided in the case. Holdings can be either express or implied.

Express holdings are easy to identify because they are announced. For example, a court might state: *We hold that driving a car at ninety miles per hour is prima facie reckless driving.* Implied holdings are usually harder to identify than express holdings because you can rely only on the court's action.

For example, a court might state: *The trial court found the defendant guilty of reckless driving without any testimony that the defendant was, in fact, operating his car in a reckless manner. Anyone who drives at ninety miles per hour is forced to dodge through traffic at a high rate of speed. This conduct is inherently reckless and endangers the well-being of others. Affirmed.*

Now study the following judicial opinion and the three proposed holdings for the case.

> ### *State v. Klein (1979)*
>
> *Casey Klein appeals his conviction for burglary. Klein was apprehended reaching into a house with ten-foot-long tree snips he had modified into a long pair of tweezers. He admitted to the police that he intended to steal a mink coat lying on a chair near an open window. Appellant klein denies that he could properly have been convicted of burglary. The maximum offense, he argues, is attempted larceny, because that crime requires only an attempt to steal the property of another. The prosecutor, however, correctly sought and won a conviction for burglary. Generally, burglary occurs only if the defendant is physically present in the house; he must actually penetrate the enclosure of the dwelling. Although the defendant in this case never entered the house, he did extend his tree snips through the window. There is no meaningful difference between the snips and his arm because the penetration by the snips was merely an extension of Klein's person. Crime has run rampant in recent decades and this type of activity must be discouraged. Burglary carries a greater penalty than attempted larceny and this penalty will more effectively deter such crimes. We therefore hold that the need to deter such activities renders the defendant's actions burglary. Affirmed.*

Answer A:

A defendant may properly be convicted of burglary during a high crime period when his conviction will deter similar actions, even if he was not physically present in the building.

Answer B:

For the purposes of burglary, three snips are the same as a human arm.

Answer C:

The protrusion of tree snips held by defendant into a dwelling satisfied the penetration element of burglary even if the defendant's body does not enter the dwelling.

The actual holding of the case is contained in Answer C. It shows how the relevant legal rules was found applicable to the facts of this case. Answer C does not justify the holding; it is simply a statement of what the court decided. This is the rule that subsequent courts will apply or distinguish. Answer A is what the court said it was holding, but not what it actually held. Deterring crime is a reason the court gave for deciding the case the way it did, but reasons are holdings are different things. The holding, again, is what the court actually decides in the case.

Answer B sounds more like a holding and less like a reason than Answer A. It does not, however, offer a very useful holding. A tree snips may be the same as a human arm, but that statement fails to explain what legal rule is involved.

C. Identify the Issue

Cases usually develop because the parties disagree over the application of one or more rules of law to a particular set of facts. The issue is the legal question that must be resolved before a case can be decided. The holdings helps identify the issue because the holding is the answer to the issue.

Now study the following judicial opinion and the three suggested issues:

Johnson v. Silk (1980)

Alice Silk and Fran Johnson, university students who had recently met, decided to use Silk's small sports car to drive to their hometown for the weekend. Silk told Johnson she would pay all their travelling expenses to repay Johnson for tutoring Silk before the midterm examination in Silk's Chinese philosophy class. Shortly after they started out, Silk lost control of her car and it struck a construction barrel on the side of the road. Johnson suffered severe injuries and brought suit against Silk to recover damages. The trial court granted Silk's motion to dismiss, and Johnson appealed. The state Automobile Guest Statute bars guest passengers from suing drivers for injuries they sustain in automobile accidents. The statute applies only if the passenger did not confer a substantial benefit on the driver that motivated the driver to provide the ride. The trial court found that Johnson was barred from recovery because she "paid nothing for the ride". The issue in this case is whether Johnson assumed the risk of her own injury by riding on a busy highway in a small sports car. Johnson tutored Silk, and she did so before the ride with every expectation of repayment. Silk owed a favor to Johnson that she felt obligated to repay, and under general principles of fairness actually was bound to repay. The Guest Statute therefore is inapplicable. Reversed.

Answer A:

Whether a passenger injured in an accident while riding in a small sport car on a busy highway is barred by assumption of risk from suing the driver of that car for damages.

Answer B:

Whether a court can disregard the Automobile Guest Statute to reach a just and fair result.

Answer C:

Whether a passenger's tutoring of a driver before a mid-term examination constitute a substantial benefit that bars application of the Automobile Guest Statute.

The court had to decide whether the Automobile Guest Statute applied to this situation. Application of the statute turned on whether the passenger conferred a substantial benefit on the driver. This is the real issue. The correct statement of the issue is Answer C.

Answer A is what the court said the issue was, but it is not what the court decided. Because the issue and the holding are so closely related, you must look elsewhere for the issue.

Answer B may be your first reaction to what happened in this case, but issues must be defined in a legal context, not a political one. Fairness is mentioned in the opinion, but it was a reason for the decision, even though the court mistakenly said it was the holding.

D. Identify the Rule

Once you have determined the issue and holding, you should identify the rule. The rule is the general legal principle relevant to the particular factual situation presented. It can be a rule fashioned by a court in a previous case, a synthesis of prior holdings in case with similar facts, or a statutory provisions.

Rules, issues and holdings are closely related. The issue is generally how the relevant rule will be applied to the specific facts of the case. The holding is the resolution of the issue, the determination of how the rule should be applied to the case.

The following examples are illustrative:

Whitman v. Whitman (1997)

James Whitman's will left all of his property to his brother George. James's wife challenged the validity of the will after James died, claiming that it did not express James's clear intent. She sought to present evidence, including her own testimony that James actually wanted to give a substantial portion of his estate to her. The trial court excluded the evidence, and we affirm. The rule in this state is that an unambiguous will is conclusive as to the testator's intent unless it would contravene law or public policy. All other evidence must be excluded. Because James's wife sought to present precisely such evidence, and the will was not ambiguous, the trial court properly ruled the evidence inadmissible. We find no legal or public policy reason to depart from the intent expressed in the will.

Identifying the rule in this case is simply because the court explained that "the rule in this state" is that an unambiguous will is conclusive as to the testator's intent. But consider this opinion:

> ### Central Credit Co. v. Smith (1989)
> Olan Computer Company began to operate as a business before it was properly incorporated. Prior to proper incorporation, the company made sales and incurred debts. Olan's creditors are seeking to hold Smith and Jones, the incorporators and sole shareholders, personally liable for these debts. A corporation does not legally exist until it has been properly incorporated. Once a business is properly incorporated, a creditor must look to the corporate entity to satisfy its claim. The trial court properly found Smith and Jones personally liable for the debts. Affirmed.

Because the precise rule used by the court is not stated here, you must identify it by inference. The legal rules stated by the court and its holding in this case help the inquiry. A corporation's legal existence begins with proper incorporation, the court said. After that time, the corporation's shareholders are not personally liable for its debts. The court also held these shareholders personally liable for debts they incurred before incorporation. The court thus applied a corollary of the rules stated: A shareholder of a corporation can be held personally liable for debts incurred when the company is not properly incorporated.

E. Identify the Facts

Once you understand the rule, holding, and issue, you will be able to identify the relevant facts of the case. After the initial reading of the case, you have a general knowledge of the facts. Now you are ready to reread them and determine which facts were important to the decision. Judicial opinion usually contain a lengthy description of the facts because the court wants the reader to understand the situation completely. You are expected to identify two kinds of facts, legally relevant facts and procedurally significant facts.

Legally relevant facts are those the court consider important in deciding the case. Sometimes these facts are events that did occur, and sometimes they are events that did not occur. These facts are outcome determinative, they effected the court's decision.

Procedurally significant facts describe at what stage in the case an error may have occurred in the lower court. These facts, which are routinely stated in appellate opinions, including the ruling of the trial court on the matter that is the subject of the appeal. Procedural facts are also important because the procedural posture of the case affects what legally relevant facts are available to the appellate court. When the parties agree on the facts, the trial court simply determines and applies the relevant law.

Consider the following opinion and factual statements:

Lost River Ditch Co. v. Brody (1923)

The defendant owns a small riparian tract on Apple Blossom Creek. In the fall of 1922 he began diverting 45,000 gallons of water a day form a pump house on that tract to a non-riparian parcel one-half mile from the stream. The defendant claimed he needed the water because he had just doubled the size of his herd. The plaintiff, who owned another riparian tract downstream on the creek, sued the defendant for damages, claiming that any diversion of water from the watershed was impermissible. Although the plaintiff was unable to prove any actual damages, the jury awarded him one dollar in nominal damages. We reverse. Diversion of water from the creek to a non-riparian tract without some evidence of damage does not provide a basis for recovery of nominal or any other damages.

Answer A:

The defendant, who owned a small riparian tract on Apple Blossom Creek, diverted 45,000 gallons of water per day in the fall of 1922 to supply water for his recently doubled cattle herd. The plaintiff, a downstream riparian owner on the same creek, sued the defendant for damages, claiming that any diversion of water from the riparian tract was prohibited. A jury awarded the plaintiff one dollar in nominal damages even though he was unable to prove actual damages. The defendant appealed.

Answer B:

The defendant, who owned a riparian tract on a creek, diverted water from the creek to a non-riparian tract. The plaintiff, a downstream riparian owner on the same creek, sued the defendant for diverting the water. The plaintiff could not show actual damages, but a jury awarded him nominal damages. The defendant appealed.

Answer B is better because it contains only those facts the court used to decide the case and those facts needed to explain what happened in the trial court. Answer B contains nothing else; it is simple and succinct. Answer A is a slightly rewritten version of the facts stated in the case. It includes interesting details, but the name of the creek, the quantity of water diverted and other details have nothing to do with the legal rule or the significant facts of this case. Answer A also omits an important fact. Because the rule applies only to water diverted to a non-riparian tract, Answer A should have stated that the water was diverted from the creek to a non-riparian tract.

F. Identify the Disposition of the Case

The disposition is simply a statement of what the appellate court did with the decision of the court below. When only two courts are involved—the appellate court and the trial court—stating the disposition is straightforward. If the courts agrees with the lower court's decision, the judgment is "affirmed". If the court believes the decision was erroneous, the judgment is "reversed".

G. Identify the Reasons and Policies

Reasons are the steps in the logical process a court uses in arriving at its holding. Reasons can be simple explanation of how a legal rule or policy is applicable or inapplicable to the case, or they can be more involved explanations of why the analysis from on area of the law is applicable to an entirely different area of law. Policies are similar to but broader than reasons. Polices are important because they define the future direction of the law.

H. Check for Congruency

Once you have some idea of the important facts, the issue, the rule of law, the holding, the disposition, and the reasons and policies, check these elements against one another to make sure they are congruent. You might test for congruency by using the following model:

1. Facts: What happened?
2. Issue: How does the law apply to these facts?
3. Rule: The Law?
4. Holding: The result when the law is applied to the facts?
5. Disposition: Did the court agree with the decision below?
6. Reasons & Policies: Justification for the result, in light of the laws and facts?

If you are using the same law and the same facts in each element, and they accurately reflect the court's decision, you have a good case brief.

I. In multiple-issue case, analyze each issue separately

If the case contains multiple issues, to analyze each issue separately can avoid confusion.

Exercis:

> ### *Roberts v. Zoning Commission (1998)*
>
> Appellant Edwin owns a parcel of land. He applied to the city Zoning Commission to rezone the parcel from R-3(single-family residential) to OI(official-institutional). The Commission denied his application, finding that all surrounding parcels are zoned for and contain single-family homes. Roberts produced evidence that the parcel was appraised at between $50,000 and $90,000 under the current zoning, but would worth $200,000 to $250,000 if rezoned.
>
> Following the denial of his rezoning request, Roberts filed this action, alleging that the Zoning Commission had taken his property without compensation, in violation of the state and federal constitutions. To demonstrate a taking, the challenger to a zoning classification has the burden of presenting clear and convincing evidence that he has suffered a significant detriment.
>
> The trial court properly dismissed the landowner's complaint because Roberts failed to meet his burden. Merely showing a disparity in the market value of property as currently zoned versus its values if rezoned is not, by itself, sufficient to establish a significant detriment. Offers for real estate depend on the method of marketing and the asking price. Because the landowner did not attempt to market the property at an asking price consistent with its value under current zoning, no significant detriment has been shown. We must bear in mind that zoning ordinances exist to ensure the greater good of the community even though specific zoning may not always be in the best interest of an individual. Affirmed.

Facts:

Rule:

Issue:

Holding:

Disposition:

Reasons and policies:

Section 3 Precedent and Stare Decisis

The concepts of precedent and stare decisis serve as important checks on the judicial freedom and ensure that the law develops in an orderly fashion.

Considerable freedom to modify legal rules and principles in accordance with social norms, views of justice and common sense. Courts look to previous decisions on similar questions for guidance in deciding present cases.

Previous decisions on similar questions are known as precedent. Reliance on precedent ensures that similar cases are decided according to the same basic principles and helps courts to process case more efficiently.

The value that surround the notion of precedent are reinforced by the principle of stare decisis. The doctrine of stare decisis states that when a court has set forth a legal principle, that court and all lower courts under it will apply that principle in future cases where the facts are substantially the same.

Precedent	Stare Decisis
Merely requires that courts look to previous decisions for guidance	Requires that a court follow its own decisions and the decisions of higher courts within the same jurisdiction

Precedent can be of two types, binding or persuasive. When the doctrine of stare decisis applies, precedent is binding and a court must reconcile the result in a given case with past decisions.

In the binding precedent, not all parts have the legal effect, only the core of the ruling theory *(Ratio Decidendi)* part is legally binding. The rest is not the legally binding part which is known collectively as *Obiter Dictum*. *Ratio Decidendi* refers to the reason for the decision.

It usually includes the material facts and reasons for the court's decision. To decide which part belongs to *Ratio Decidendi* is often the difficulty in distinguishing cases.

The following two cases illustrate how precedent and stare decisis function.

Brainerd v. Harvey (1982)

The plaintiff is an elderly man who lived in a small building in a high crime area. The building had poor lighting on its front porch and a continuously unlocked outer door. As the plaintiff was about to enter the building one night, the outer door was jerked open by an unknown youth who had been hiding inside. The youth struck and robbed the plaintiff. The plaintiff brought suit against the landlord, but the trial judge granted the defendant's motion for a directed verdict of no cause of action.

We reverse. We have from time to time held that persons are liable for negligently exposing others to foreseeable criminal activities and this is such a case. The inadequate lighting and locks were physical defects in a common area of the building under the landlord's control; this would be a far different case if the building had not contained such defects. The landlord's negligence in failing to repair them made it more likely than not that the plaintiff would be victimized by a criminal attack.

The trial court also erred in refusing to grant the plaintiff a jury trial. The plaintiff demanded a jury trial. He did not waive that right by waiting until the pretrial conference to make his demand. Remanded for a jury trial.

Douglas v. Archer Professional Building, Inc. (1986)

In 1978, a mental health clinic leased and began occupying an office on the fifth floor of the Archer Professional Building. About two years later, an outpatient at the center stabbed Carol Douglas, a physician with an office in the building, while both of them were riding in the building's elevator. Dr. Douglas brought suit against the owner of the building. At trial, the director of the clinic testified that the stabbing was the first such incident in his ten years of experience with such programs. There was also testimony that before the incident other tenants in the building had voiced concern over use of the elevators and the stairwells by the clinic's patients. Dr. Douglas won a jury verdict for $115,000 in damages. We affirm.

We stated in Brainerd v. Harvey that landlords are liable for damages caused when they negligently expose others to foreseeable criminal attacks in common areas of

> buildings they lease. In both this case and Brainerd, the attack occurred in an area of the building under then landlord's control and used by all tenants. Just as the landlord in Brainerd knew or should have known about the absence of adequate lighting and locks in the apartment building, the defendant here knew or should have known about the potentially dangerous condition in the professional building. When the landlord is informed by his tenants that such a condition exists, he has a duty to investigate and take any possible preventive measures. The jury could properly find that the landlord's failure to do so was negligence.
>
> Fisher, J., dissenting. The court here imposes unwarranted and unreasonable burdens on landlords by vastly extending their potential liability. In Brainerd v. Harvey, we expressly limited the landlord's liability to his failure to detect and repair their dangerous physical conditions in common areas of leased buildings. Unlike the front door, this professional building had no physical defect that enabled the assault to occur. In Brainerd, we also limited liability to foreseeable criminal attacks, rather than those based merely on the subjective fears of some tenants in the building. The majority opinion suggests a medieval fear of persons who receive mental health care and will impede the state's goal of returning mental patients to the community.

After deciding the first case in 1982, the same state appellate court was presented with an opportunity four years later to expand the scope of the rule to cover a different factual situation. These two cases illustrate the tension between change and stability that is the central to the study and practice of law.

Section 4 Judicial Opinions

Courts rarely state explicitly that they are overruling a prior case. Appellate courts are supposed to decide only as many issues as are necessary for the disposition of a case.

Trial courts are responsible for finding facts and applying the law, while appellate courts have greater authority to modify and expand the law. The doctrine of stare decisis has worked well over centuries.

Because it gives case law stability and predictability, while at the same time allowing for gradual change.

Although the US Supreme Court and the highest courts of the state have the power to overrule prior decisions, they hesitate to do so.

When a court overrules a case, the court nullifies a prior decision as precedent. It usually occurs when the same court in a later case establishes a different rule on the same point of law involved in the earlier case. When a court reverses a case, an appellate court sets aside the decision of the lower court.

In Plessy v. Ferguson, *163 U.S. 537(1896)*, the US Supreme Court approved separate but equal accommodations for different races on trains. Using Plessy as precedent, the separate but equal doctrine was extended to other public accommodations, including schools.

In Brown v. Board of Education, *347 U.S. 483(1954)*, the US Supreme Court overruled Plessy v. Ferguson, holding that separate but equal doctrine in public schools was unconstitutional.

Over the 58 years between the two decisions, changes in society made the United States Supreme Court decide that Plessy should be overruled.

Judges write the judicial opinions to explain the reasons and policies for the decisions of the case in a particular way. Generally, the judicial opinion usually begins with the jurisdiction of court to explain the court's authority for hearing the case. Then it states the procedural history and facts of the case. After that, it states the discussion about the analysis of case with applying legal rules and reasons or relevant policies. The last part states the proposition of law and the disposition. In this part, different types of opinions would be introduced.

The type of opinion in a case is important:

1. Majority opinion: an opinion agreed upon by at least the majority of the judges deciding the case. Usually, one judge writing the opinion and other judges who agree with the opinion join it. If the minority of judges disagree with the disposition or the reasons, they may write separate opinions or express their thinking on this case. Even though there are concurring or dissenting opinion, a majority opinion is the disposition of the case that the lawyers need to study.

2. Plurality opinion: a case decision agreed upon by more judges than any other opinion, although less than a majority. Normally, plurality decisions of a state supreme court are not binding under the doctrine of stare decisis. Such an opinion may be easily overruled in appeal.

3. Concurring opinion: an opinion in which a judge agrees with the result reached in an

opinion but for different reasons. A concurring opinion is not the disposition of the case and it is not binding. It sometimes may limit the majority opinion to some extent. However, the lawyers often find instructive values from this opinion when analyzing cases in the future.

4. Dissenting opinion: written by a judge who disagree with the result reached by the majority opinion. It expresses the judge's reasons for the disagreement. One or more judges may join a concurring or dissenting opinion. It is not binding but it may reflect the weakness of the majority opinion. Therefore, the losing party may find supports from the dissenting opinion. It may become the majority of the court in the future dealing, the lawyers may predict the future development of law from dissenting opinion.

5. *Per curiam* opinion (Latin): by the court, describes an opinion backed by all the judges in a particular court and usually with no one judge's name. Generally, when the case is easy and there is no contradiction, the court as a whole and gives the unanimous opinion. Occasionally, if the issue is so sensitive that the judge is not willing to be named on the opinion, the court may also give a *per curiam* opinion.

6. En banc opinion (French): All the judges of a court participating in a case all together, rather than individually or in panels of a few. It usually appeared in the cases of great importance.

7. Memorandum opinion: a concise opinion in a simple case expressing the holding of the court. Generally, a memorandum opinion does not contain long reasons.

Chapter 6
Legal Rule Analysis

案例的研读、法律争议的解决及法律文书的写作（如合同条款的设计）等离不开对法律规则的认识和分析。法律规则往往以一定的逻辑结构将单个或多个条件、行为方式和产生的关系或结果纳入。一项法律规则的产生可能源自于某个案件、法规或条例。关于某一特定主题的普通法通常是随着时间的推移而发展的，因为后来的案件增加或完善了这一规则。对法律规则结构及其逻辑架构的分析具有重要的实践意义。

法律规则的不同要素体现了立法者的规则导向和价值取向。规则要素建立起法律事实和法律结果的相互关系。细分要素将进一步明确规则适用的情形。当然，法律规则并不局限于单一的法律规定或案例发展。综合多项法律规定或经典案例，将有助于提升研习者对特定规则的理解。

A rule can be derived from a single source, such as a case, a statute, or a regulation. It can also be derived from a combination of sources: a series of cases, or a statute and cases that interpret the statute.

Section 1　Elements of Rules

A legal rule may contain several parts. These parts, elements, sub-elements, results and exceptions are put together in a certain way.

A. Elements

An element of a rule describes a factual condition that must exist for a rule to apply. Each element can stand alone as a single independent unit.

Consider the following rule regarding a driver's license:

A person shall be issued a driver's license if he or she meets all of the following requirements:

1. *The person must complete an application for a license.*
2. *The person must be at least 16 years old of age.*
3. *The person must be a resident of the state.*
4. *The person must pass all examination requirements for a license.*
5. *The person must pay the appropriate fee.*

This rule has five elements. Notice that each element can stand alone; each can exist without reference to the others.

The elements of a legal rule are most commonly combined in one of three ways.

1. The rule may require all of the elements to be met.
2. Only one of the elements must be established.
3. All of the elements are relevant, but only some, not all are needed.

B. Results and Relationship to Elements

The result of a rule describes what will happen when the elements of the rule are established as required.

The driver's license rule states that a person "shall be issued a driver's license" if the elements of the rule are met.

The single word "shall" links the result to the elements of the rule and tells you that the result must follow if the elements are established.

Considering the following examples, explain how a rule establishes a different link between the elements of a rule and the result.

1. Any person who is convicted of two or more moving traffic violations within six months may not operate a motor vehicle until the person completes a driver safety course.

2. Any person who is convicted of driving under the influence of alcohol may be sentenced to imprisonment not exceeding thirty days or required to pay a fine not exceeding $2,500.

C. Exception in a Rule

Sometimes legal rules have exceptions that are often indicate with words such as "unless", "provided that", or "however". Recall the rule on a driver's license:

A person shall be issued a driver's license if he or she meets all of the following requirements:

1. *The person must complete an application for a license.*

2. The person must be at least 16 years old of age.

3. The person must be a resident of the state.

4. The person must pass all examination requirements for a license.

5. The person must pay the appropriate fee. If, however, the person has three or more convictions for driving under the influence of alcohol, from this or any other state, a driver's license may not be issued.

D. Sub-Elements

Sometimes an element of a rule is defined by one or more sub-elements. Consider the tort of battery as defined in the Restatement (Second) of Torts §13 (1965).

An actor is subject to liability to another for battery if

(a) he acts intending to cause a harmful or offensive contact with the person of the other or a third person, or an imminent apprehension of such a contact, and

(b) a harmful contact with the person of the other directly or indirectly results.

Under subsection (a), two requirements are apparent:

(1) the defendant must "act" and (2) the defendant must intend to cause a certain kind of contact.

Under subsection (b), there also appear to be two requirements: (1) a "harmful contact" must occur; and (2) the contact must be the "result" of the defendant's act, there must be a causal connection between the defendant's act and the harmful contact.

Finally, subsection (a) and (b) are connected with the word "and". Thus, these elements are conjunctive; the act, the intent, the contact, the causal connection must all be present for a battery to be committed. The consequence of this rule is clear: If all of elements are established, the defendant is liable for battery.

Exercises:

Read the following rule:

To establish intentional infliction of emotional distress the plaintiff must show that the defendant's conduct was intentional towards the plaintiff, the conduct must be extreme and outrageous, there must be a causal connection between the defendant's conduct and the plaintiff's mental distress, and the plaintiff's mental distress must be extreme and severe.

Please consider:

1. How many elements does this rule contain?

2. Do any of the elements have sub-elements?

3. What result if the elements of the rule are established?

4. Are there any exception to the rule? If so, when do they come into play? What result if an exception to the rule exists?

Section 2   Developing a Rule from Multiple Sources

Legal rules do not always appear fully formed in a single case or statute. The common law on a particular topic often develops over time, as later cases add to or refine the rule. It is therefore important to be able to derive a rule from a body of law, as well as from a single source. The process of combining sources into a coherent statement of the law is referred to as "synthesis".

Assume that you are defending a client who has been charged with aggravated menacing. You need to determine the meaning of the word "knowingly" as used in the statute.

Section §290.30 Aggravated Menacing

No person shall knowingly cause another to believe that the offender will cause serious physical harm to the person or property of the other person, the other person's unborn, or a member of the other person's immediate family. Whoever violates this section is guilty of aggravated menacing.

State v. Rosenby (1991)

Appellant Ronald Rosenby appeals his conviction for aggravated menacing. At trial, Clarice Penn testified that she terminated her relationship with appellant in July 1989 because appellant had physically abused her. Penn also testified that on the evening of October 15,1989, appellant drove to her home and screamed at her from his vehicle for nearly one-half hour, and then threatened to "take her to the grave with him".

Appellant contends that the elements of aggravated menacing were not met because the statement "take her to the grave with him" was not accompanied by any kind of physical movement or attempt to carry out the threat. It is sufficient if the offender "knowingly" causes the victim to believe the offender will carry his threat into execution. The jury could reasonably conclude that appellant "knowingly caused" Penn to believe that he would kill her when he approached her at home and told her that he would "take she to the grave with him". Affirmed

State v. Wentz (1996)

Defendant appeals his conviction for aggravated menacing, arguing that the evidence was insufficient to establish all elements of the charge.

Fifteen-year-old Nick Hampton testified that Defendant told him to relay a message to his mother, Ronnie Hampton, that "she's messing with the wrong person if she tries to bust him for anything, she'll be hurting."

During a subsequent encounter two days later, Defendant asked Hampton if he had relayed the message to his mother. Ronnie Hampton testified that her son told her what Defendant had said, and that she interpreted the message as a threat of "serious physical harm, like he was going to come after me and shoot me or something".

Defendant argues that there was insufficient evidence to establish that he acted "knowingly" because he did not threaten Hampton's mother personally and therefore did not "knowingly cause her to believe that he would harm her". Defendant knew that Hampton lived with his mother, asked him to take her a message, and then verified that the message had been delivered. We hold that Defendant acted with the requisite knowledge when he directed Nike Hampton to deliver a threatening message to a member of his own family, his mother Ronnie Hampton.

Conviction affirmed.

State v. Huffman (2003)

Appellant appeals his conviction for aggravated menacing. We reverse. The Country Child Support Enforcement Agency intercepted Appellant's income tax refund as a result of child support arrearages. Appellant called a caseworker, Josephine Manning, to complain about the amount of money he had been ordered to pay to his former wife and said, "I can't even afford to eat. Maybe I should just kill her, maybe that will end it all." Manning reported this conversation to her supervisor, Ned Turner, who reported the incident to the police and warned Appellant's former wife about the comment Appellant had made. After a bench trial.

Appellant was found guilty of Aggravated Menacing and placed on probation.

Appellant contends that it was against the manifest weight of the evidence for the court to find that he acted "knowingly" because it was not probable that his statement to Manning would be conveyed to his former wife. A person acts knowingly when he is aware his conduct will probably—that is, more likely than not—cause a certain result. For

> appellant to have spoken knowingly, therefore, it must have been "more likely than not" that Manning would relate Appellant's statement to his former wife.
>
> Manning did not know Appellant's former wife. She testified that she did not call the police and did not expect that her supervisor would. In light of this testimony, reasonable minds could not conclude that it was "more likely than not" that Manning would convey Appellant's statements to his former wife. Accordingly, we reverse his conviction.

After reading the cases, you have been asked to write a memo regarding the meaning of the word "knowingly". Your problem is that the three decisions are each based on different factual situations and different rationales.

Consider the two possible suggestions, which statement of the rule would you find most helpful?

Answer A:

To be found guilty of aggravated menacing, the defendant must "knowingly cause another to believe that the offender will cause serious physical harm to the person or property of the other person, the other person's unborn, or a member of the other person's immediate family". State Code §290.30. The meaning of "knowingly" depends on the manner in which the threat is delivered. See, e.g., *State v. Rosenby; State v. Wentz; State v. Huffman.*

Answer B:

To be found guilty of aggravated menacing, the defendant must "knowingly cause another to believe that the offender will cause serious physical harm to the person or property of the other person, the other person's unborn, or a member of the other person's immediate family." State Code §290.30. The "knowingly" element is established if the defendant (1) delivers the threat directly to the victim, *State v. Rosenby*; (2) delivers the threat to a member of the victim's family, *State v. Wentz*; or (3) delivers the threat to a third party who defendant believes will "more likely than not" convey the threat to the victim, *State v. Huffman.*

Both answers cite all the relevant authorities. Answer B is better, however, because it states the rule clearly. The reader knows immediately that the elements can be satisfied in three different ways and can easily check the rule against a new set of facts to see if the element is met. Answer B provides brief summary of each of the three cases in a way that provides considerable precision about how the courts have understood "knowingly". Answer A is weaker because it conveys much less information about that element. It implies that there is more to the word "knowingly" than meets the eye, but it is much too vague to give the reader a clear understanding of the rule and its requirements.

Exercise:

How to understand the process of "synthesis"?

Chapter 7
Common Law Analysis

普通法系中的法律分析遵循逻辑体系发展的过程。成文法和判例法在普通法体系中的共存也导致了法律适用的不同方法。判例法原则的适用是从一组事实到另一组事实进行推理的过程,而成文法的适用需要一种演绎推理方法,将一般原则适用于个别案件的事实。

普通法系法律分析的主要方法是类比和区分。其中,案例分析的核心内容是围绕争议焦点展开。

争议焦点(issue)是争议双方向法院提出并必须由法院解决的问题。争议事实与确定案件适用的法律规则有密切关系。为确定适用的法律规则,首先应确定原告在审判法庭上对被告的诉讼事由,以及确定该诉讼事由所需的要素。

先例原则要求法院遵循有类似事实情况的先例,如果有此类先例,并且该案例不能被充分区分时,法院必须将该先例的判决按比例适用于待判决的案件事实。当研究先例是否或如何适用于案件时,普通律师必须首先研究司法意见中包含的理由。同时,在进行普通法推理时,法院须考虑其裁决对未来法律发展的影响。

Section 1　Legal Reasoning Process

Legal analysis is a sequential process. First, one must find all authority relevant to the problem. Some areas of the law are governed wholly by case law; other areas are governed by constitutions, statutes, court rules, or administrative regulations, as applied and interpreted by the courts.

Here are the usual steps in legal analysis:

When searching case law, one must search for a prior case decided by the highest possible court in the jurisdiction with the same issue as presented in the legal problem you are researching and with as similar as possible material facts. Any case found should be further

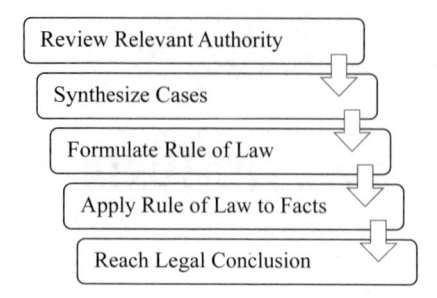

```
Review Relevant Authority
   ↓
Synthesize Cases
   ↓
Formulate Rule of Law
   ↓
Apply Rule of Law to Facts
   ↓
Reach Legal Conclusion
```

researched to make sure it has not been later heard and decided by a higher court or overruled or that there is not a more recent case from the same or a higher court. When researching constitutions, statues, court rules and administrative regulations, one must search for an applicable primary sources and any case law applying or interpreting the primary source. A statute should be further researched to make sure it has not been amended, repealed or held unconstitutional. Constitutions, court rules, and administrative regulations should be further researched to make sure they have not been amended. There are deductive reasoning and reasoning by analogy as two major reasoning for law analysis.

- Deductive Reasoning

Deductive reasoning involves reasoning from the general (rule) to the specific (the impact of the rule on a particular fact pattern). The first step in deductive reasoning is to identify the rules that may apply to a particular fact pattern. A rule that may apply is referred to as the major premise. The second step is to state the facts in terms of the rule. This statement is called the minor premise. The facts must be weighed in the light of the language of the rule to formulate the minor premise. In other words, should the language of the rule to formulate the minor premise. In deductive reasoning, major premise serves as the basis for a logical deduction, the facts or arguments upon which a conclusion is based.

Minor premise serves as the basis for a logical deduction weighed in light of the major premise. The facts or arguments upon which a conclusion is based.

- Reasoning by Analogy

Reasoning by analogy first involves finding a past case with facts that appear to be similar to the case presently being decided. No two fact patterns are identical, even if they involve similarly situated parties or what appears to be the same issue. Therefore, there will always be similarities and differences between the two fact patterns. The second step is to compare the facts of the two cases to determine which facts are similar and which facts are different. The third step is to determine whether the facts of the two cases are so substantially similar that the past case should determine the result in the present case. If the facts in the two cases are substantially different, then the result in the present case might differ from the result in the past case. In examining factual differences and similarities, one must determine whether the similarities or differences are more significant. A few similarities between crucial facts in the two cases may outweigh numerous differences in unimportant facts.

Exercises:
1. What are the features of common law analysis?
2. How to evaluate steps in legal analysis?

Section 2　Identifying and Selecting Issues for Analysis

An issue is one that is presented to and must be resolved by the court. Such an issue should identify the facts of the case as they relate to the law and the clearly applicable rule of law. In order to find the applicable rule of law, one should first identify the plaintiff's cause of action against the defendant in the trial court, and the elements necessary to establish that cause of action. These elements constitute the legal rules governing the dispute. A case may contain more than one issue, and there may be several disagreements about the law that the appellate court is called upon to resolve. If this is the case, each issue should be analyzed separately in accordance with the requirements described above describing each issue.

The first step in solving a legal problem is to select questions that require analysis from the broad range of questions suggested by the facts of the case. First, focus only on questions within the scope of the problem. Second, identify all relevant questions.

Here is the case for discussion:

Fred Brookson, a life long resident of Klamath Falls, Oregon, contacted with your firm to see whether he can file suit against Wendell Carter for injuries sustained as a result of an incident that occurred in southern Oregon. About three month ago, Brookson and his wife, Ellen, from whom he is now separated, participated in a demonstration concerning recent acts of violence against doctors practicing in a local abortion clinic. The demonstration occurred on a wharf extending into the Coos River. A group of people, including Wendell Carter, gather around the demonstrators and began to heckle them. The two groups exchanged remarks and eventually the hecklers threw rocks and bottles at the demonstrators. When Carter threw a rock that struck and injured Ellen, Fred became angry and approached

Carter. Carter said he regretted injuring Ellen because he had been aiming at Fred. The two men exchanged heated remarks. Then without any provocation, Carter pulled out a knife, screamed and lunged at Brookson, intending to stab him. As Brookson jumped back to avoid being injured, he almost bumped into an unidentified demonstrator. The demonstrator, who apparently thought he was being attacked, struck Brookson several times and seriously injured him. Both Brooksons required medical treatment, and Fred Brookson required and extended hospital stay. His medical expenses exceed $128,000; his estranged wife's expenses were approximately $9,000. Both have lost weight, exhibit chronic anxiety, and have periods of severe insomnia. Carter grew up in California but has spent the last three years attending college and living in Oregon.

§1332. Diversity of Citizenship

(a) The district courts shall have original jurisdiction of all civil actions where the matter in controversy exceeds the sum or value of $75,000, exclusive of interest and costs, and is between

(1) Citizens of different states;

(2) Citizens of a state and citizens or subjects of a foreign state;

(3) Citizens of different states and in which citizens or subjects of a foreign state are additional parties; and

(4) A foreign state ... as plaintiff and citizens of a state or of different states.

For the purpose of this section ... an alien admitted to the United States for permanent residence shall be deemed a citizen of the state in which such an alien is domiciled.

Diversity Jurisdiction Elements Chart		
Element	Facts of Our Case	Element Met?
Civil action		
Amount in controversy exceeds $75,000		
Parties fall into one of the following categories		
(1)		
(2)		
(3)		
(4)		

Each of these elements is plausibly met in a case. An elements chart, such as the one below, shows whether the individual elements of a rule are, may be, or are not applicable to the facts of your case.

Diversity Jurisdiction Elements Chart		
Element	Facts of Our Case	Element Met?
Civil action	Action by private citizens to recover damages	Yes
Amount in controversy exceeds $75,000	Medical cost exceeds $128,000	Yes
Parties fall into one of the following categories		
(1)	Parties are an Oregon resident and a person who grew up in California but lived in Oregon for the past three years as a college student	May be
(2)	^	No
(3)	^	No
(4)	^	No

Also, for a tort claim, the possible rule is as follows:

A defendant commits battery when he (1) acts ; (2) intends to cause a harmful or offensive contact with the plaintiff or a third person; and (3) thereby causes (4) a harmful or offensive contact with the plaintiff. There is also a chart for reference.

Element	Facts of Our Case	Element Met?
Acts	Carter lunged at Brookson with a knife	Yes
Intends to cause a harmful or offensive contact with the plaintiff or a third person	Carter wanted to stab Brookson	Yes
Thereby causes	Brookson almost bumped into an unidentified demonstrator to avoid Carter, and demonstrator then beat Brookson	May be
A harmful or offensive contact with the plaintiff	Brookson was severely beaten by an unidentified demostrator	Yes

Also, do not forget to exclude givens (legal questions with clear answers) from detailed discussion and separate issues and sub-issues if there is any.

Exercises:

1. Please describe the process for selecting issues.

2. Please explain possible issues related to jurisdiction.

Section 3   The Method of Common Law Analysis

The common law develops cautiously because the principles of precedent and stare decisis render it comfortably with the familiar and less comfortable with unknown.

The judges and lawyers in civil law countries seek guidance from enacted statutes in practicing law; however, a common law court looks to previous decisions on similar issues for guidance in deciding present cases. The previous decisions on similar questions are known as precedents, and the rule that requires the court to follow precedents is called the rule of precedent. The rule of precedent is one of the fundamental notions of the common law system, which is based on the idea that an issue, once properly decided, should not be decided again.

The primary methods of common law analysis are analogy and distinction. Every case involving the possible application of a common law rule involves two basic questions:

1. How are the decided cases similar to my client's case?

2. How are the decided cases different from my client's case?

Your client, Arthur Dooley, a tenant in a large apartment building, had several grievances with the building's manager, Otis Fremont. Dooley designed a one-page flier in which he asserted, "Fremont has a long record of criminal convictions as a landlord." Fremont had received three notices of violation from the local housing commission in the past two years for inadequate lighting and locks. The commission had then threatened to seek a court order requiring correction of the violations, but dropped the matter when Fremont made the necessary repairs. Fremont has no criminal record.

Dooley made 200 copies of the flier at his print shop for distribution to other tenants in the building. On his way back from the print shop, Dooley met Fremont by chance and, after a lengthy conversation, they settled their differences. The fliers were not mentioned. Although Dooley intended to destroy the fliers when he returned to his apartment, he was struck by a teenager riding a skateboard and the fliers were scattered by the wind. Other persons read many of the fliers, and Fremont filed suit for libel.

There are relevant cases. All are from the highest appellate court of the state.

White v. Ball (1966)

Ball appeals from a libel judgment awarded to White and two other employees of the R & T Construction Company. Ball had hired the company to remodel his home. The judgment was based on a letter written by Ball to the company president shortly after the work was completed, in which Ball accused the employees of stealing a valuable watch.

The first issue on appeal is whether the letter has been intentionally published. As a general matter, libel consists of the international publication of false statements about a person that humiliates the person or subjects him to the loss of social prestige. All that is necessary for publication to occur is the delivery of the defamatory matter in written or other permanent forms to any person other than the one libeled. It is the receipt by a third person that makes the statements so damaging. Because the president of the company, a third person, received and read the letter, the trial court was correct in finding that there was intent to publish.

The second issue is whether the letter was false. On this issue, the trial court erred. A statement is false if the gist, the sting, of the matter is false.

Minor inaccuracies in the statement are not sufficient to show that it is false. In this case, the accusation against the employees was, in a technical sense, false. None of the employees took the watch. But a male friend of one of the employees took the watch when he picked her up at the end of the workday. Because of the relationship between the employee and the thief, we believe that the letter has been substantially accurate. Reversed.

Simmons v. Deluxe Plaza Hotel (1988)

The manager of the defendant hotel wrote Simmons a letter falsely accusing Simmons of staying in the hotel, failing to pay for the room, and taking several articles from the room. The manager was mistaken as to the culprit's identity, so the letter was false. The letter was addressed to Simmons personally and sent by the certified mail. Simmon's wife signed for the letter at his residence and read it. The question on appeal is whether the trial court correctly ruled that the letter was not intentionally published. The evidence shows the manager considered it possible that some third person might receive the letter, though he did not know Simmons was married. This falls far short of a showing that he was reasonably chargeable with appreciation or knowledge of the likelihood that the letter would be opened and read by another. A mere conceivable possibility or chance of such eventually is not sufficient to demonstrate intent. Affirmed.

Libel Elements Chart		
Element	**Facts of Our Case**	**Element Met?**
Intent to publish	**Dooley wrote and printed 200 fliers, intending to distribute them to Fremont's tenants. They were published accidentally after Dooley no longer intended to publish them.**	**May be**
Publication	Fliers were ready by third persons.	Yes
Of a false statement about a person	Fliers said Fremont had a long record of criminal convictions as landlord. Fremont was cited three times in two years by Housing Commission and corrected violations to avoid the court order. Fremont had no criminal record.	May be
That humiliates the person or	Fliers said Fremont had a long record of criminal violations.	May be
Subjects him to the loss of social prestige	**Fliers said Fremont had a long record of criminal violations.**	**Yes**

Analyzing one of these sub-issues, whether the "intent to publish" rule should be applied to these facts.

Intent to Publish case briefing chart			
	Our Case	**White**	**Simmons**
Facts	Dooley designed and printed copies of a flier to distribute to tenants in his apartment building. After he decided not to publish them, they were released by accident.	The defendant wrote a letter to a company president containing allegations about his employees. The company president received and read the letter.	The defendant wrote a letter that was addressed personally to the plaintiff and sent by the certified mail. The plaintiff's wife read the letter. The defendant thought it possible that someone else would read the letter, but did not know the plaintiff was married.
Holding		There was intent to publish.	There was no intent to publish.
Reasons & Policy		Receipt by a third person makes statements damaging.	Intent requires reasonable knowledge or appreciation that a letter will likely be ready by another. Mere conceivable possibility or chance that a third person would read a letter does not constitute intent.

This case briefing chart helps focus the intent sub-issue. It extracts the facts, holdings, reasons and policies of the cases concerning this sub-issue.

The following outline provides a method for analyzing any other common law issue:

1. Determine how the facts of the decided cases support your client's position.

2. Determine how the facts of the decided cases support your opponent's position.

3. Determine how the reasons and policies of the decided cases support your client's position.

4. Determine how the reasons and policies of the decided cases support your opponent's position.

5. Evaluate the strength of your client's case.

Exercise:

Please depict the first four steps in the above method by using the chart below.

	Intent to Publish Analysis Chart	
	Why the element is met (the opponent's argument)	Why the element is not met (our client's argument)
Facts		
Reasons & Policies		

Section 4 Statutory Analysis

Statutory law is the law promulgated by the legislature with the authority to make laws, and the executive with the authority to make rules to implement the statutes. The laws enacted by the legislature and the executive are referred to as Acts of Parliament, legislation, statutes, regulations, ordinances, or enactments.

The co-existence of both statutory law and case law in common law system also leads to different approaches to the application of law. While the application of case law principles is a process of reasoning by analogy from one set of facts to another, the application of the statutory law requires a deductive method of reasoning, which applies a general principle to the facts of an individual case.

Statutory analysis is the process of determining how statues apply to a given situation and what effect they may have. Statutory analysis differs from common law analysis because it focuses on the meaning of legislative pronouncements rather than judicial ones. The purpose of the analysis is to determine whether the category described by the text does or does not apply to your client's situation.

Statutory analysis can best be understood by use of a hypothetical problem.

Until the recent election, members of the Liberal Party held all seven seats on the Grand View City Council. The conservatives, who promised in the recent election to significantly recorder the city's budget priorities, now outnumber the Liberals on the Council by four to three. Your client, Joshua Smith, an important member of the Liberal Party, learned that the four Conservative members plan to meet privately within several weeks to write their proposed budget. This budget will then be presented to the full Council. The budget goes into effect once it has been adopted by a majority of the Council. Council meetings require a quorum of five. The Conservatives told Smith that neither he nor any other member of the public would be permitted to attend the private meeting. The four members do not constitute any formal Council committee.

Is the Conservatives' position lawful under the state Open Meetings Act?

The Act provides:

Sec.1 Purpose. It is vital in a democratic society that public business be performed in an open and public manner so that the citizens shall be advised of the performance of public officials and of the decisions that are made by such officials in formulating and executing public policy. Toward this end, this chapter is adopted and shall be construed.

Sec.2 Definitions. As used in this Act:

(a) "Meeting" means the convening of a public body for the purpose of deliberating toward or rendering a decision on a public policy.

(b) "Public body" means any state or local legislative body, including a board, commission, committee, subcommittee, authority, or council that is empowered by law to exercise governmental or proprietary functions.

Sec.3 All meetings of a public body shall be open to the public and shall be held in a place available to the general public.

The state court of appeals has decided one case concerning this statute:

Time-Journal Co. v. McPhee (1977)

The appellant, Times-Journal Co., brought an action seeking declaratory and injunctive relief against McPhee and the other members of the Bedford Board of Education, claiming that they had violated, and planned to continue violating, the state Open Meetings Act by closing a series of "preliminary" and "informal" meetings to the public. The trial court granted the defendants' motion to dismiss on the ground that no formal actions were taken at these meetings, even though they were attended by the entire board. Therefore, the court reasoned, they were not "meetings" within the meaning of the act. We reverse.

Section 2 (a) defines "meeting" as the convening of a public body "for the purpose of deliberating toward or rendering a decision on a public policy".

Every step in the decision-making process, including the decision itself, is necessarily part of the deliberation that the legislature intended to affect by the enactment of the statute before us. "Preliminary" and "informal" meetings are necessarily part of that deliberative process.

A "meeting" occurs under section 2 (a) if there is a convening of public body for deliberating towards or rendering a decision on a public policy.

The following charts depict this analysis.

Meeting Elements Chart		
Element	**Facts of Our Case**	**Element Met?**
Convening	Four Council members meet privately	Yes
Of a public body	Four member Conservative majority of City Council; five required for quorum	May be
For the purpose of: deliberating toward or	Will write proposed budget, which will then be presented to full Council	Yes
Rendering a decision	Will write proposed budget, which will then be presented to full Council	May be
On a public policy	Budget	Yes

The following principles provide a method for resolving issues.

1. Determine how the language of the statute, and the facts of any cases interpreting the statute, support your client's position.

2. Determine how the language of the statute, and the facts of any cases interpreting the statute, support your opponent's position.

3. Determine how the policies of the statute, and the policies of any cases interpreting the statute, support your client's position.

4. Evaluate the strength of your client's position.

Exercise:

Please make a chart analysis for "public body" element from the above case.

Public Body Elements Chart		
Element	*Facts of Our Case*	*Element Met?*
State or local legislative body, including a board, commission, committee, authority, or council		
Empowered by law to exercise governmental or proprietary functions		

Chapter 8
Dispute Resolution-Litigation

民事诉讼制度的一个基本功能是为因权利和义务而发生纠纷的民事主体提供一种有序、可靠和可预测的解决纠纷的手段。

作为民事纠纷的公力救济手段，诉讼的实质是由国家审判机关，在纠纷主体的参加下，处理特定的社会纠纷的一种权威和有效的机制。诉讼是法院以国家审判权确定纠纷主体双方之间的民事权利义务关系，并以国家强制执行权迫使纠纷主体履行生效的判决和裁定。诉讼具有严格的规范性，必须严格地按照法律规范进行。

本章重点介绍中国民事诉讼体系，包括中国民事诉讼与刑事诉讼、行政诉讼的区分，诉讼程序与仲裁程序的区分，诉讼程序与调解的区分。就民事诉讼的原则而言，本章就中国民事诉讼法规定的基本保障原则和民事诉讼特有原则，以及涉外因素的诉讼原则进行简要的介绍。

Section 1　Definition of Litigation

A. Definition from Law Dictionaries

Litigation, would be defined as the process of carrying on a lawsuit (the attorney advised his client to make a generous settlement offer in order to avoid litigation) or a lawsuit itself (several litigations pending before the court).

In litigation you either take the initiative or you stand on the defensive, and your attack or defense must be supported upon one or both of these two elements. The aim of an intelligent preparation is to secure for your client a superior advantage over his adversary on the law, or on the facts, or on both. If by prudent provision you can be stronger on the facts under the law, you will win, or if your case be in the proper construction of the law, which you can show, it may be by great research and exhaustiveness of presentation to be for you, again you have the preponderance. But if you can present superior combinations, both of law and fact, then you are doubly safe. The right preparation of a case is scientific, and its object is to present for client at the trial, on those points of controversy, which is cardinal or controlling. A little observance of trials and arguments will give the reader a clearer insight into the subject than many more pages, however plainly written and filled it might be to overflowing, with illustrations. As the student observes the argument after the evidence is all in, he will often detect for himself, the preponderance of the prevailing party, and he will likewise, while hearing discussion of legal questions, begin to see before the judge delivers his opinion, who will win it and how. Napoleon's saying, that the art of war consisted all in being the stronger on a certain point, is accepted as a maxim. So in litigation, there are turning points, either of law or fact where superiority will win for the party who has it.

B. Definition from Leading Foreign Scholars

Essentially, the law of civil procedure is the law governing the civil litigation process. The term "civil litigation" is not one that enjoys a precise and generally accepted definition. Fundamentally, it involves the process of enforcing private rights and obligations, and the resolution of disputes concerning such rights and obligations, through the mechanism of a court proceeding. Potentially, civil litigation may relate to virtually any kind of dispute submitted to a court, about any subject in which one party is claimed to have committed a private wrong against another party.

One basic function of the civil litigation system in any country is to provide to parties who are engaged in a dispute over entitlements and obligations, a means of resolving that dispute in a way that is orderly, reliable and predictable. Without such a mechanism, many such disputes could lead to violence. As an alternative to self-help, courts impose upon a dispute the authoritative power of the state in the pursuit of a reasoned, principled decision. Fundamentally, the law of civil procedure concerns the method by which parties who are in dispute with each other may determine and enforce their respective substantive rights (and their respective corresponding obligations) through an orderly process of litigation. It is inherent in a democratic society that members of the general public will view their conflicting aspirations as amounting to rights of entitlement. Where the aspirations of different members of that society cannot be reconciled so that each person can enjoy his or her claimed entitlement to its full extent, conflict is an inevitable consequence.

In any civil action of interpleader or in the nature of interpleader, a district court may issue its process for all claimants and enter its order restraining them from instituting or prosecuting any proceeding in any state or the United States court affecting the property, instrument or obligation involved in the interpleader action until further order of court. Such processes and order shall be returnable at such time as the court or judge thereof directs, and shall be addressed to and served by the United States marshals for the respective districts where the claimants reside or may be found.

Such district court shall hear and determine the case, and may discharge the plaintiff from further liability, make the injunction permanent, and make all appropriate orders to enforce its judgment.

Very few cases proceed through all of these stages of litigation. In 2015, less than 2 percent of cases that were resolved in the federal district courts actually went to trial. Most were resolved before reaching the stage of a pretrial conference, by voluntary dismissal, dismissal by the court on various grounds, settlement, or summary judgment. The federal courts resolve many cases, but try very few of them.

Exercise:

Please explain general function of civil procedure law.

Section 2 General Introduction of Chinese Civil Procedure System

A. Definition from Leading Chinese Scholars

Civil litigation refers to all kinds of litigation activities carried out by the People's Court, the parties and other participants in the process of trying civil cases, and all kinds of litigation activities generated by these activities.

Litigation activities include not only the trial activities of the people's court, such as case acceptance, investigation and evidence collection, application of coercive measures, making judgments, etc., but also the litigation activities of litigation participants, such as the plaintiff's prosecution, the defendant's defense or counterclaim, and the witness's appearing in court to testify, etc. However, not all the activities of the people's court are litigation activities. For example, the activities of the collegial panel of the court to discuss cases and the activities of the judicial committee to discuss cases are not litigation activities, but activities within the court, which are regulated by the organic law of the court. Litigation activities must be the activities that the court and litigation participants can have litigation relationship in the process of litigation. If the court accepts the plaintiff's action, it will serve a copy of the complaint to the defendant within the legal time limit, which is a kind of litigation activity in the process of litigation. Litigation activities are closely related to litigation.

Litigation relationship refers to the relationship of litigation rights and obligations among the people's court and all litigation participants in the process of litigation. The People's Court is always a party in the litigation relationship, and it has a relationship with the other party in the litigation relationship. For example, after the plaintiff has filed a lawsuit, the court will accept it and serve a copy of the plaintiff's complaint to the defendant within the legal time limit, so that the court has litigation relations with the plaintiff and the defendant respectively.

It can be seen that litigation is composed of litigation activities and litigation relations. Litigation activities can produce, change or eliminate litigation relations, which are manifested through litigation activities. At the same time, these litigation activities and litigation relations are stipulated in the civil procedure law. In other words, they are litigation activities and litigation relations according to law.

The meanings of civil procedure in the PRC has two respects. First, it refers to the litigant activities, e.g., the actions of a party to institute a lawsuit or to participate in the proceedings, the action of a witness to provide evidence, and the action of an expert to make an expert evaluation as well as the activities of the people's court to try the case. Second, it refers to the legal relations, e.g., the relations among the people's court, the plaintiff and the defendant, and the relations among the people's court and other litigant participants.

B. Distinction with Criminal Procedure

Chinese civil procedure like most of the countries in this world is different from criminal procedure which has its own procedure law.

Traditionally and practically, people's courts shall follow the principle of "criminal case first and civil case second", i.e., if a criminal case is found in trying a civil case, the criminal part shall be given to a trial following criminal procedure, and civil procedure shall suspend until the criminal judgment is given if it cannot be separately and independently carried out.

In Chinese criminal procedure, however, there is a special procedure of incidental civil action, in which a victim or the people's procuratorate on behalf of the state and a collective property shall have the right to claim their damages caused by the criminal conduct of the criminal defendant during the course of the criminal proceeding. In the incidental civil action, the provisions of CCPL shall apply, but the criminal defendant cannot be against the provisions of criminal procedure limiting the personal freedom of the criminal defendant. An incidental civil action shall be heard together with the criminal case. Only for the purpose of preventing excessive delay in a trial of the criminal case may the same judicial organization, after completion of the trial of the criminal case, continue to hear the incidental civil action.

By the way, the Tort Law of the PRC, which was promulgated on 26 December, 2009, stipulates in Article 4 that where an infringer shall assume administrative liability or criminal liability for the same conduct, it shall not cause him to undertake the tort liability according to the law.

However, where his assets are not enough to undertake his tort liability, administrative liability and/or criminal liability for the same conduct, the tort liability shall be first assumed.

C. Distinction with Administrative Procedure

Unlike civil procedure dealing with the litigation between the equal subjects, Chinese administrative procedure is a kind of procedure dealing with the litigation that a citizen, a legal person or any other organization considers that his or its lawful rights, and interests have been infringed upon by a special administrative act of an administrative organ or its personnel. Compared with civil procedure, Chinese administrative procedure is distinct in many ways, e.g., its object is always the specific administrative act; the defendant can only be the administrative organ; a people's court shall not apply conciliation in handling an administrative case; and the defendant shall not collect evidences during the proceedings.

D. Distinction with Arbitration

Arbitration in the PRC has its own laws and rules, though there are close links with civil procedure. All Chinese arbitration commissions are the members of the China Arbitration Association, which shall formulate arbitration rules according to the Arbitration Law and the Civil Procedure Law (Article 15 of the Arbitration Law). The validity of an agreement for arbitration and the lawfulness of an arbitration award might be decided by the people's court according to the CCPL. The PRC adopted its Arbitration Law in August 1994, which is only formally adjusted in 2009 to make the number of some provisions identical with those in the CCPL. Before that law, China divided arbitration into two types: domestic and foreign-related arbitration.

Domestic arbitration carried out the system of arbitration and judicial judgment, i.e., any party who refused to accept the award of arbitration might bring a lawsuit for the same dispute in a competent people's court. Foreign-related arbitration carried out the system that the award is final, i.e., any party of the arbitration should be bound by the award and could not bring a lawsuit for the dispute in a people's court any more. After that law, arbitration in China was unified to be the system that the award was final one. Now, a system of a single and final award shall be practiced for arbitration (Article 9 of the Arbitration Law). If the parties have concluded an arbitration agreement and one party institutes an action in a people's court, the people's court shall not accept the case (Article 5 of the Arbitration Law). If a party applies for arbitration to an arbitration commission or institutes an action in a people's court regarding the same dispute after an arbitration award has been made, the arbitration commission or the people's court shall not accept the case.

In China, there are two foreign-related arbitration commissions now. One is China International Economic and Trade Arbitration Commission (CIETAC) and the other is the Maritime Arbitration Commission, both of which have their own arbitration regulations respectively and have gained their world-wide reputation. Besides that, there have been many arbitration commissions established in the PRC since 1994, which have their own regulations following the regulations of the Arbitration Law. Since the Arbitration Law does not prohibit other arbitration commissions to rule the foreign-related cases, many of the former domestic arbitration commissions began this practice, though the CIETAC is still the most well-known arbitration commission in China.

There are some possible exceptions to an arbitration agreement. And an arbitration agreement shall be null and void under one of the following circumstances:

(1) The agreed matters for arbitration exceed the range of arbitrable matters as specified by law.

(2) One party that concluded the arbitration agreement has no capacity for civil conducts or has limited capacity for civil conducts.

(3) One party coerced the other party into concluding the arbitration agreement (Article 17 of the Arbitration Law).

According to Article 58 of the Arbitration Law, if a party concerned has evidences to prove one of the following circumstances, he may apply for the cancellation of arbitral award with the intermediate people's court at the place where the arbitration commission resides:

(1) There is no agreement for arbitration.

(2) The matters ruled are out of the scope of the agreement for arbitration or the limits of authority of an arbitration commission.

(3) The composition of the arbitration tribunal or the arbitration proceedings violate the legal proceedings.

(4) The evidences on which the ruling is based are forged.

(5) Things that have an impact on the impartiality of ruling have been discovered

concealed by the opposite party.

(6) Arbitrators have accepted bribes, resorted to deception for personal gains or perverted the law in the ruling.

When the people's court verifies one of the aforesaid circumstances after examination by a collegial panel, the arbitral award should be ordered to be cancelled by the court. In addition, the people's court shall cancel the arbitral award if it holds that the award goes against the public interests. The CCPL provides different conditions for a people's court to reject enforcing the arbitral award in domestic cases and foreign-related cases. Commonly in Articles 237 and 274 of the CCPL, the people's court shall, after the examination and verification by a collegial panel, make a ruling not to allow the enforcement of the award rendered by an arbitral organ of the PRC, if the party against whom the application for enforcement is made furnishes proof that:

(1) the parties have not had an arbitration clause in the contract or have not subsequently reached a written arbitration agreement;

(2) the composition of the arbitration tribunal or the procedure for arbitration was not in conformity with the statutory procedure (in domestic cases) or the rules arbitration (in foreign-related cases); or

(3) the matters dealt with by the award fall outside the scope of the arbitration agreement or which the arbitral organ was not empowered to arbitrate.

Besides the provisions, the CCPL provides one additional condition for not enforcing the arbitral award of a foreign-related case in Article 274:

The respondent is not notified to appoint an arbitrator or of the conduct of arbitration procedure or fails to present its case, which is not attributable to the fault of the respondent. Meanwhile, Article 237 provides the following conditions as the statutory circumstance of not enforcing the arbitral award for the domestic cases:

(1) The evidence for rendering the award is forged.

(2) The opposing party withholds any evidence to the arbitral institution, which suffices to affect an impartial award.

(3) When arbitrating the case, any arbitrator commits embezzlement, accepts bribes, practises favouritism for personal gains, or renders the award by bending the law. If the people's court determines that the enforcement of the award goes against the social and public interest of the country, the people's court shall make a ruling not to allow the enforcement of the arbitral award (Articles 237 and 274 of the CCPL).

If the enforcement of an arbitral award is disallowed by a ruling of a people's court, the parties may, in accordance with a written arbitration agreement reached between them, apply for arbitration again; they may also bring an action in a people's court (Articles 237 and 275 of the CCPL).

There is special arbitration in terms of labour disputes and rural land contract disputes. In accordance with the Labor Dispute Mediation and Arbitration Law (the LDMAL) of 29 December 2007 and the Law on the Mediation and Arbitration of Rural Land Contract Disputes (the LMARLCD) of 27 June 2009, these two types of arbitration shall carry out different principles other than the Arbitration Law that the arbitration award is final.

According to Article 47 of the LDMAL, an arbitral award shall be final only for cases where: (1) a dispute over the recovery of labour remuneration, medical expenses for a work-related injury, economic indemnity, or compensation, in an amount not exceeding the twelvemonth local monthly minimum wage level, and (2) a dispute over the working hours, breaks and vacations, social insurance, arising from the execution of state labour standards. Besides these cases, an employee, who disagrees to an arbitral award as provided for in Article 47 of the LDMAL, may bring an action in the people's court within fifteen days after receiving an arbitral award (Article 48 of the LDMAL).

According to Article 2 of the LMARLCD, the disputes over the contracted management of rural land include disputes arising from the conclusion, fulfilment modification, cancellation and termination of rural land contracts; disputes arising from the sub-contract, lease, interchange, transfer, holding of shares and other means of turnover of contracted management rights to rural land; disputes arising from the withdrawal and adjustment of the contracted land; disputes arising from the confirmation of contracted management rights to rural land; disputes arising from impairment to the contracted management rights to rural land; and other disputes over contracted management of rural land as prescribed in law and regulations. However, the disputes arising from requisition of collectively owned land and the compensations therefore do not fall within the scope of acceptance by the rural land contract arbitration commission; they may be settled by means of administrative reconsideration or lawsuits. The arbitration over the cases of rural disputes does not need an arbitration clause. Article 48 of the LMARLCD stipulates that where a party is dissatisfied with the arbitral award, he may lodge the people's court within thirty days from the date on which he receives the arbitral award. If he does not lodge a lawsuit within the time limit, the arbitral award shall become legally effective thereupon.

E. Civil Procedure and Conciliation

It is a distinct characteristic of Chinese civil procedure to stress that the people's courts shall conduct conciliation (mediation) for the parties on a voluntary and lawful basis in trying civil cases(Article 9 of the CCPL).

However, there are two types of conciliation in China. The conciliation in the people's court is different from that of the people's conciliation. The people's conciliation is a special system outside the people's court and litigation to resolve disputes and shall be carried out under direction of the people's conciliation committees.

According to Article 16 of the CCPL of 2007, the people's conciliation committees are mass organization to conduct conciliation of civil disputes under the guidance of the grassroots level people's governments and the basis level people's courts. The people's conciliation committee shall conduct conciliation for the parties according to the law and on a voluntary basis. The parties concerned shall carry out the settlement agreement reached through conciliation, those who decline conciliation or those for whom conciliation has failed or those who have backed out of the settlement agreement may institute legal proceedings in a people's court. If a people's conciliation committee, in conducting conciliation of civil disputes, acts contrary to the law, rectification shall be made by the people's court. All these principles remain and got detailed regulations in the Peoples Mediation Law as effective of January 2011.

In 2012, the people's conciliation was strengthened in the new CCPL. In the end of the People's Mediation Law, Article 33 stipulates that after a mediation agreement is reached upon mediation by a people's mediation commission, when necessary, the parties concerned may jointly apply to the people's court for judicial confirmation within thirty days after the mediation agreement becomes effective, and the people's court shall examine the agreement and confirm its effect in a timely manner.

Subsequently, the CCPL of 2012 set up a section confirming the effectiveness of Mediation Agreement upon judicial acknowledgement. Article 194 stipulates that, to apply for judicial confirmation of a mediation agreement, both parties to the mediation agreement shall, in accordance with the People's Mediation Law and other laws, jointly file an application with the basic people's court of the place where the mediation organization is located within thirty days from the effective date of the mediation agreement. In addition, Article 195 stipulates that, after accepting an application, if the application complies with legal provisions upon examination, the people's court shall issue a ruling to affirm the validity of the mediation agreement, and if one party refuses to perform or fails to fully perform the mediation agreement, the opposing party may apply for enforcement to the people's court; or if the application does not comply with legal previsions upon examination, the people's court shall issue a ruling to dismiss the application, and the parties may, through mediation, modify the mediation agreement or reach a new mediation agreement and may also institute an action in a people's court.

However, the conciliation in the people's court was also strengthened in the CCPL of 2012. Although it has been the practice in China, there is not an article so clear as Article 122 to stipulate that where conciliation is appropriate for the civil dispute involved in an action instituted by a party in a people's court, conciliation shall be conducted first, unless the parties refuse to participate in it. It is also important to read this article under the principle of voluntary and lawful conciliation stipulated in Article 9 of the CCPL.

The same principle shall also be carried out in the Enforcement Procedure of the CCPL. Article 230 stipulates that where, during enforcement, both sides reach a settlement agreement, the enforcement personnel shall record the provisions of the settlement agreement in the enforcement transcripts, to which both sides shall affix their signatures or seals. It is clear that this kind of settlement agreement shall not be the result of a fraud or under duress. In that case, the people's court may, upon application of a party, resume the enforcement of the original effective legal document.

Exercises:

1. Please list some progresses that Chinese Civil Procedure Law has made.
2. Please distinguish civil litigation from arbitration.

Section 3 The Sources of the Civil Procedure Law

Although there are some academic debates in the PRC on how far the extension the civil procedure law shall be, it is generally agreed that the civil procedure law in China refers to the norms regulating activities of civil litigation and legal relations of litigation. According to the sense of generally-accepted theory and practice, the civil procedure law in China mainly refers to the civil procedure law and the relevant judicial explanations given by the Supreme People's Court.

There are other laws and regulations relating to the civil procedure law, which are mentioned above; however, it is generally agreed by Chinese scholars and practitioners that these laws and regulations do not directly regulate the civil litigation within the people's court and they are not within the scope of the civil procedure law in this narrow sense.

Judicial explanations are not a form of statute law in Chinese legal system. Chinese legal tradition does not adopt the idea of precedent laws which are enacted by courts and judges. However, judicial explanations, especially those given by the Supreme People's Court, are of great importance in implementing laws. The people's courts at various levels shall also follow the judicial explanation in their adjudicative activities, including civil procedure.

It is true that many provisions in a law and even the law itself in the PRC largely come originally from judicial explanations. A very good example of this practice is the Special Procedure of Maritime Litigation of the PRC promulgated on December 1999. This law was made upon the experiences gained from a series of judicial explanations for maritime litigations 1986.

The characteristics and fundamental guarantees of (administration of justice in civil matters can be seen in the fundamental principles of the CCPL rally speaking, the fundamental principles of the CCPL can be divided into two categories: the principles reflecting the fundamental guarantees based upon the Constitution and the Organic Law of the Peoples Court (OLPC) and the principles directing the characteristics of civil procedure. For foreign parties, there are two particularly important principles: the principles of equality and the principle of reciprocity.

A. The Principles Reflecting the Fundamental Guarantees

The principles reflecting the fundamental guarantees are established by the Chinese Constitution and they apply not only to civil proceedings but also to other types of proceedings.

1. The principle that the adjudicative power over civil cases can only be exercised by people's courts

The principle that the adjudicative power over civil cases can only be exercised by people's courts is provided by the Constitution as well as the CCPL. In the PRC, the people's courts are the judicial organs of the state, and the people's courts shall exercise judicial powers with respect to civil cases (Article 6 of the CCPL) and whoever engages in civil litigation within the territory of the PRC must abide by the CCPL (Article 4 of the CCPL). Although civil disputes can be handled by people's government and people's conciliation committees, the settlements cannot prevent the people's courts from jurisdiction. In the case of arbitration, any awards of arbitration cannot be deemed as a result of adjudicative authority. The people's court shall have power to cancel the award based upon the circumstances expressly stipulated in the CCPL and upon the request of a party. In case that any party fails to perform the award of an arbitration, the other party may apply the people's court to enforce it according to the CCPL.

2. The principle that the people's courts are independent in adjudicating civil cases

The principle that the people's courts are independent in adjudicating civil cases is guaranteed by the Constitution. The people's courts exercise judicial power independently, in accordance with the provision of the law, and are not subject to interference by any administrative organ, public organization or individual. According to the Constitution and the CCPL, it is indeed that the people's courts shall be responsible and report to the legislative authorities which created them (Article 128 of the Constitution), and that the people's procuratorates shall have the right to exercise legal supervision over civil proceedings (Article 14 of the CCPL). The adjudicative activities of the people's courts cannot be interfered by either of them, as long as they are carried out according to the law.

Unlike other Western countries, the independent adjudication of the people's courts means the independence of a people's court at large and not that of a judge personally. It is the people's court at large that can enjoy the independence of adjudicative power. Within a people's court, there are certain organs where a judge shall work in and whose decision he might have to obey, as are mentioned below in details. However, a judicial reform has been carried out in China, in which a judge shall take more personal responsibility for his judgments. The new tendency is taking place in China and moving towards an exciting direction.

3. The principle taking facts as basis and law as criterion

The principle taking facts as basis and law as criterion is a famous legal dictum in Chinese legal vocabulary and is expressly provided in the CCPL for trying civil cases (Article 7). According to the request of taking facts as basis in trying civil cases, the people's courts shall avoid being subjective, lopsided and outwardly in ascertaining the fact of a civil case.

Taking the law as criterion requires the people's courts to distinguish right from wrong, to affirm civil rights and obligations and to impose sanctions for civil wrongs only according to the law enacted by the state.

4. The principle that all litigants are equal in implementation of law

The principle that all litigants are equal in implementation of law is guaranteed by the Constitution as well as the CCPL. All citizens of the PRC are equal before the law (Article 33 of the Constitution). According to this principle, the people's court shall not be partial to or discriminate against any party because of its ethnic status, race, sex, occupation, social background, religious belief, education property status, or ownership. It is also the requirement of this principle that the people's court shall equally apply the law for the litigants of aliens and stateless persons and shall not discriminate against them because of their nationalities.

5. The principle of native spoken and written languages

The principle of native spoken and written languages is particularly important for the litigants of the minority nationalities. The PRC is a unitary multinational state. There are fifty-six minority nationalities living together in this country, of whom the nationality of Han consisting of more than 90% of the population. All nationalities have the freedom to use and develop their own spoken and written languages (Article 4 of the Constitution). Citizens of all nationalities shall also have the right to use their native spoken and written languages in civil proceedings (Article 11 of the CCPL). In order to guarantee this might, the CCPL further stipulates that where minority nationalities live together in one area, the people's courts shall conduct hearings and issue legal documents in the spoken and written languages commonly used by the local nationalities, and that the people's courts shall provide translations for any participant in the proceedings who is not familiar with the spoken or written languages commonly used by the local nationalities.

6. The principle of public trial

The principle of public trial is a basic system in the CCPL. In the people's courts, civil cases shall be tried in public, except for those that involves state secrets or personal privacy or are to be tried otherwise as provided by the law. The case of divorce or the case involving trade secrets may not be heard in public if a party so requests. The public trial means that a trial shall be opened to the public and shall allow people to be the auditor and public medium to report it. This system may provide people with an opportunity to supervise adjudicative activities and to have a lesson how the law to be implemented.

B. The Principles Directing the Characteristics of Civil Procedure

The principles reflecting the fundamental guarantees are not the unique principles of the civil procedure. There are some principles directing the characteristics of civil procedure.

The principles directing the characteristics of civil procedure contain the principle of equal litigation rights, the principle of conciliation, the principle of arguing for a party himself, the principle of dealing with one's own rights, the principle of procuratorate supervision, the principle of supporting the injured party to bring an action in a people's court and the principle of people's conciliation.

1. The principle of equal litigation

The principle of equal litigation is expressly stipulated in the CCPL. The parties in civil litigation shall have equal litigation rights. The people's court shall, in conducting the trials, safeguard their rights, facilitate their exercising the rights, and apply the law equally to them (Article 8 of the CCPL).

The principle of equal litigation is not the same as the principle that all litigants are equal before implementation of law. The former means that the parties in civil procedure equally enjoy and exercise litigation rights, and the later means that the people's court shall equally apply the law to the parties in a civil case.

The principle of equal litigation requires that the parties of both sides shall have equal litigation statue in the civil proceeding. Any party cannot enjoy more right than the other party does in civil procedure, no matter whether he is on behalf of a kind of special rights such as the state-owned interests or not. Correspondingly, both parties shall also bear equal litigation obligations. The peoples court shall initiate to inform the litigants of what kinds of litigation right they can have in trying a civil case. It is particularly important for the litigants who are short of legal knowledge.

2. The principle of conciliation

The principle of conciliation refers to the conciliation in the people's court. According to the CCPL, the people's courts shall conduct conciliation for the parties on a voluntary and lawful basis in trying civil cases. However, judgments shall be rendered without delay if a conciliation fails (Article 9). Conciliation can be exercised in all kinds of civil cases and all kinds of procedures, except for the cases which shall adopt special procedure, summary procedure for hastening recovery of a debt, procedure for publicizing public notice for assertion of claims, for the case of affirming a contract invalid as well. Conciliation in the people's court is aimed to simplify and fasten civil proceed and to help both parties avoid hurting their feelings after litigation. Both conciliation and judgment are the methods for the people's court to resolve a civil dispute and judgment is the backing of conciliation. If no agreement is reached through conciliation or if either party backs out of the settlement agreement before the conciliation statement is served, the people's court shall render a judgment without delay.

3. The principle of arguing for a party himself

The principle of arguing for a party himself means actions are entitled in the trials by the people's courts to argue for themselves. It is because of this principle that the civil procedure in the PRC is inclined towards the adversary procedure.

This principle shall run through the whole proceedings of a civil litigation procedure, not only in the phase of court debate. Both parties shall be allowed to argue not only in the procedure of first instance, but also in second instance and the procedure for trial supervision as well.

The form of the debate is mainly oral, but the written one is also possible. The topic of the debate is primarily the civil dispute itself. In addition, the issues in the procedural aspect can be also argued.

4. The principle of dealing with one's own rights

The principle of dealing with one's own rights means that the parties are free to deal with their own civil rights and litigation rights in the way they prefer within the scope provided by the law (Article 13 of the CCPL). In 2012, the CCPL adds the principle of good faith to Article 13 as the paragraph, which means that the principle of good faith will govern the whole area of civil proceedings and any activities of all parties and even the court itself.

Like the principle of arguing, this principle shall also run through the whole proceedings. The principal expression of this principle can be seen in the following circumstances: the party can decide at his own discretion on whether to bring a lawsuit in a people's court, when his civil interests were violated or disputed, after a proceeding begins, a plaintiff who may abandon his claim or a defendant who may acknowledge parties may become reconciled by themselves; a litigant may decide at his own discretion on whether to file an appeal against a judgment or a ruling of first instance of a local people's court and to apply to a people's court for executing the legally effective judgment or ruling. It is obvious that the litigant's dealing activities as such are of great impact to occurrence, change or termination of a civil proceeding.

However, the party's dealing rights are limited "within the scope provided by the law" according to the CCPL. This limitation means that the parties dealing rights are not absolute and might be subject to the interference of the state, if any litigation activities are against law or violate the civil interests of the state or others. For example, the people's court shall not approve the settlement agreement of both parties for reconciliation, and the trial shall continue, if the agreement is against law.

It is also due to this reason that the people's court shall not be interfered by the litigation conduct of either party during the course of trying the civil case. Although a party may apply for withdrawing a lawsuit after bringing a suit but before propouncing the judgment, for example, it shall still depend upon the order of the people's court whether the application shall be permitted.

5. The procuratorate supervision

That the people's procuratorates shall have the right to exercise legal supervision over civil procedure is stipulated in Article 14 of the CCPL. Here, civil procedure refers to the whole civil procedure including the activities of enforcement and is no longer limited only in proceedings. This is an expansion of the procuratorate supervision. According to the principle of procuratorate supervision, the people's procuratorate shall have the right to supervise civil proceedings. The traditional supervision right is to lodge a protest in the people's court which made the judgment people's procuratorate believe wrong. However, the legal effect of a protest is to trigger the retrial procedure in the people's court. A successful protest will not give the people's procuratorate the right to bring a civil lawsuit or participate in a civil proceeding.

In 2012 CCPL, the method of the procuratorate supervision expanded from the protest to the procuratorate recommendation. The procuratorate recommendation can refer to the one for retrial or the one for any violation of law by judges in any trial procedure other than the trial supervision procedure. However, the procuratorate recommendation retrial is not like the protest in three aspects: First, it will not definitely trigger the retrial procedure while the protest will. Second, it is filed by a people's procuratorate to the people's court at the same level while the protest can only be filed against the erroneous decision made by the people's court at the lower level. Third, the procuratorate recommendation for retrial against an effective legal decision can only be filed by the local people's procuratorate while the protest can be filed by the Supreme People's Procuratorate, too.

In order to strengthen the power of the people's procuratorate, Article 210 of the CCPL stipulates that a people's procuratorate may, as necessary for offering procuratorial recommendations or filing a protest to perform its duty of legal supervision investigate and verify relevant information from the parties or parties to a case. The Supreme People's Procuratorate issued the Provisional Regulations on Supervision of Civil Proceedings on 18 November 2013 to regulate the activities of protest and recommendation. Article 15 of the CCPL stipulates that where an act has infringed upon the civil rights and interests of the state, a collective organization or an individual, any state organ, public organization, enterprise or institution may support the injured unit or individual to bring an action in a people's court.

The principle of supporting the injured party to bring an action in a people's court provides therefore various units, who does not have any direct interests in the case, with the right to support the injured units or individual.

C. The Principles Particularly Applicable to Foreign Litigants

In addition to the principles reflecting the fundamental guarantees and the principles directing the characteristics of civil procedure, there are two principles particularly important to foreign litigants: the principle of equality and the principle of reciprocity.

1. The principle of equality

Article 5 of the CCPL stipulates that aliens, stateless persons, foreign enterprises and organizations that bring suits or enter appearance in the people's courts shall have the same litigation rights and obligations as citizens, legal persons and other organizations of the PRC.

2. The principle of reciprocity

If the courts of a foreign country impose restrictions on the civil litigation rights of the citizens, legal persons and other organizations of the PRC, the people's courts of the PRC shall follow the principle of reciprocity regarding the civil litigation rights of the citizens, enterprises and organizations of that foreign country.

It is generally agreed that the principle of reciprocity applies not only to the restrictions due to the provisions of the civil procedure law, but also to the judicial immunity due to a diplomatic agreement, an international custom or an international agreement.

Exercises:
1. Explain principles of Chinese Civil Procedure Law.
2. Please list general considerations for foreign litigants in Chinese Civil Procedure Law.

Chapter 9
Dispute Resolution-Arbitration

　　仲裁是指发生争议的双方当事人，根据其在争议发生前或争议发生后所达成的协议，自愿将该争议提交中立的第三方进行裁判的争议解决制度。仲裁具有灵活性，当事人可以选择管辖争议实质的法律、仲裁地点、仲裁机构和仲裁员，还可以做出一系列的其他决定，以决定仲裁的管辖范围、程序组成和实际行为。仲裁的一裁终局能够快速解决争议，同时还具有保密性。这些优点使仲裁越来越占据着纠纷解决途径的重要地位。本章从仲裁的法律含义、相关国际公约及其评论或解释报告对仲裁的性质、一般的程序和仲裁裁决等内容进行了分析。

　　《承认与执行外国仲裁裁决公约》(即《纽约公约》)的生效使得仲裁裁决具有了全球可执行性，往往成为跨境争议解决的重要途经。仲裁机构往往会推出仲裁示范条款，以便当事人选择与使用，并通过优化仲裁服务来获取竞争上的优势。本章也列举了部分全球知名的仲裁机构的示例条款，直观地展现了争议解决条款的设计，读者也可从中发现以仲裁作为争议解决方式时需要重点关注的仲裁地、准据法及仲裁员等内容的约定。最后，本章介绍了中国《仲裁法》及相关司法解释中有关仲裁委员会、仲裁协议等规定，以及《内地与香港特别行政区法院就仲裁程序相互协助保全的安排》，帮助读者对于中国仲裁法律体系形成清晰的认识。

　　Arbitration is a voluntary and consensual process and is widely used for the resolution of international disputes. One of the key advantages of arbitration is its flexibility. Parties can choose the law governing the substance of the dispute, seat of arbitration, arbitration institution (if one is used) and the arbitrators, and also make a range of other decisions that shape the jurisdictional scope, the procedural make-up and practical conduct of the arbitration. The choices made by the parties can result in important legal and tactical advantages.

　　Within the universe of Alternative Dispute Resolution (ADR), arbitration enjoys a prominent status. If the disputing parties need a binding decision but do not want to go to court, arbitration is the preferred dispute resolution method.

The identification of arbitration as it is constituted in legal lore is not very difficult. There is a near consensus of judicial utterance and statutory provision posing it as a process for hearing and deciding controversies of economic consequence arising between parties. It begins with and depends upon an agreement of the parties to submit their claims to one or more persons chosen by them to serve as their arbitrator.

In defining arbitration, it has been common in the law reports for judges to expand upon its general outline as set out above and to refer to it as a substitute for litigation in the courts. Thus: "Arbitration is the submission of some disputed matter to selected persons, and the substitution of their decision or award for the judgment of the established tribunals of justice." "Broadly speaking, arbitration is a contractual proceeding, whereby the parties to any controversy or dispute, in order to obtain an inexpensive and speedy final disposition of the matter involved, select judges of their own choice and by consent submit their controversy to such judges for determination, in place of the tribunals provided by the ordinary processes of law." Similarly, "an arbitration is a substitute for proceedings in court"; also, "an agreement to arbitrate is really an agreement between parties who are in controversy, or look forward to the possibility of being in one, to substitute a tribunal other than the courts of the land to determine their rights."

To make the content of the arbitration more clearly understood, the following analysis will be carried out from the following aspects.

Section 1 Definition from Law Dictionaries

Editor-in-chief of *Black's Law Dictionary* Bryan A. Garner, the world's leading legal lexicographer, has assembled an unmatched roster of academic and practicing contributors who have vetted every term for accuracy. Therefore, the interpretation of arbitration and related terms following in the *Black's Law Dictionary* is authoritative and credible.

"Arbitration": A dispute-resolution process in which the disputing parties choose one or more neutral third parties to make a final and binding decision resolving the dispute.

"Ad hoc arbitration": (1) Arbitration of only one issue. (2) An arbitration that does not involve an arbitration provider or institution to administer the proceeding.

"Arbitration agreement": An agreement by which the parties' consent to resolve one or more disputes by which the parties' consent to resolve one or more disputes by arbitration. An arbitration agreement can consist of a clause in a contract or a stand-alone agreement and can be entered into either before a dispute has arisen between the parties (a pre-dispute arbitration agreement) or after a dispute has arisen between the parties (a post-dispute arbitration agreement or submission agreement).

"Arbitration award": A final decision by an arbitrator or panel of arbitrators.

"Foreign arbitration award": An arbitration award that is made in a country other than the country in which enforcement of the award is sought. For example, if France is the arbitral seat, the award is made in France. When a party seeks to enforce the award in the United States, the award is considered a foreign award in the United States.

"Arbitration clause": A contractual provision appointed to hear and decided a dispute according to the rules of arbitration.

"Arbitration provider": An organization that provides administrative services for parties in arbitration. The services provided typically include promulgating standard-form procedural rules, maintaining panels of arbitrators, providing administrative services in support of arbitral proceedings, and acting as appointing authority, if necessary. The term "arbitration provider" is most commonly used when discussing domestic arbitration, the more usual term for international arbitration being arbitration institution.

"Arbitrator": (1) A neutral person who resolves disputes between parties, esp. by means of formal arbitration. (2) A neutral decision-maker who is appointed directly or indirectly by the parties to an arbitration agreement to make a final and binding decision resolving the parties' dispute. Parties agree to have their dispute resolved by either a sole arbitrator or three arbitrators (referred to as an arbitral panel in domestic arbitration or an arbitral tribunal in international arbitration).

"Arbitration may be defined as a method for the settlement of disputes and differences between two or more parties, whereby such disputes are submitted to the decision of one or more persons specially nominated for the purpose, either instead of having recourse to an action at law, or, by order of the court, after such action has been commenced."

"A recourse to arbitration was common in medieval England. But the courts did not look very favourably on a practice which tended to diminish their jurisdiction; and when they were asked to enforce the awards made by arbitrators against recalcitrant parties to an arbitration, they got many opportunities of laying down rules as to the conditions of the validity of these awards, as to the modes of entering them, and as to the conduct of arbitrators, which, at the end of the medieval period, were beginning to make the law as to arbitrators a very technical and not a very reasonable body of law. Its complexity was increased in the succeeding centuries; and, though some of the less reasonable medieval rules were eliminated, it became more elaborate and remained very technical, whilst the growing complexity in the law of pleading made it increasingly difficult to be sure that a disputed award would be enforced. In 1698 the Legislature made a salutary change in the law as to the method of entering awards, but it was not till the legislation of the 19th century that the manifold complexities and irrational technicalities of the common law as to arbitration were reformed, and the law assumed its modern form."

"Arbitration can be extremely informal or highly formal. It can be non-binding informal procedures, and apply customary norms or intuitive notions of justice. Or it can resemble a court proceeding with formal adversarial presentations and the application of substantive rules of law to achieve a binding judgment."

Exercises:

1. Is there any similarities from definitions of arbitration?
2. Please summarize the advantages of arbitration.

Section 2   International Conventions

Arbitration plays an important role in the field of cross-border dispute resolution due to its flexibility, efficiency and confidentiality. The emergence of relevant international conventions is conducive to meet the needs of the parties to arbitration. Meanwhile, it promotes arbitration and circulation of arbitral awards in the world. It is helpful to have a better understanding of arbitration through the analysis of international conventions.

A. Convention on the Recognition and Enforcement of Foreign Arbitral Awards (New York Convention)

Article 1.2: The term "arbitral awards" shall include not only awards made by arbitrators appointed for each case, but also those made by permanent arbitral bodies to which the parties have submitted.

B. UNCITRAL Model Law on International Commercial Arbitration

Article 2: (a) "Arbitration" means any arbitration whether or not administered by a permanent arbitral institution; (b) "arbitral tribunal" means a sole arbitrator or a panel of arbitrators; (c) "court" means a body or organ of the judicial system of a state.

Article 7: "Arbitration agreement" is an agreement by the parties to submit to arbitration all or certain disputes which have arisen or which may arise between them in respect of a defined legal relationship, whether contractual or not. An arbitration agreement may be in the form of an arbitration clause in a contract or in the form of a separate agreement.

C. The 1961 European Convention on International Commercial Arbitration

Article 2: For the purpose of this Convention,

(a) the term "arbitration agreement" shall mean either an arbitral clause in a contract or an arbitration agreement being signed by the parties, or contained in an exchange of letters, telegrams, or in a communication by teleprinter and, in relations between states whose laws do not require that an arbitration agreement be made in writing, any arbitration agreement concluded in the form authorized by these laws;

(b) the term "arbitration" shall mean not only settlement by arbitrators appointed for each case (ad hoc arbitration) but also by permanent arbitral institutions;

(c) the term "seat" shall mean the place of the situation of the establishment that has made the arbitration agreement.

D. Inter-American Convention on International Commercial Arbitration (Panama Convention)

The Governments of the Member States of the Organization of American States desired to conclude a convention on international commercial arbitration. Therefore, they reached an important consensus on making the Inter-American Convention on International Commercial Arbitration.

Sadly, there is no basic interpretation of arbitration terms in the convention, but the convention includes more practical operations.

E. Inter-American Convention on Extraterritorial Validity of Foreign Judgments and Arbitral Awards (Montevideo Convention)

The Governments of the Member States of the Organization of American States considered that the administration of justice in the American States required their mutual cooperation for the purpose of ensuring the extraterritorial validity of judgments and arbitral awards rendered in their respective territorial jurisdictions when Montevideo Convention had been made.

However, the whole convention concludes 14 articles. All of them explain the specific operation instead of making a clear definition like the Inter-American Convention on International Commercial Arbitration (Panama Convention).

Exercises:

1. What are the main function of New York Convention?
2. Please explain the influence of UNCITRAL Model Law.

Section 3   Commentary/Explanation Report

The corresponding commentary or explanation report of the international convention also plays a very important role in clarification. It helps readers get full understanding of various legal documents.

A. Convention on the Recognition and Enforcement of Foreign Arbitral Awards

UNCITRAL considers the New York Convention to be one of the most important United Nations treaties in the area of international trade law and the cornerstone of the international arbitration system. Since its inception, the Convention's regime for recognition and enforcement has become deeply rooted in the legal systems of its contracting states and has contributed to the status of international arbitration as today's normal means of resolving commercial disputes.

The genius of the New York Convention is to have foreseen, and made provision for the progressive liberalization of the law of international arbitration. Article VII (1), which governs the relationship between the Convention and other applicable treaties and laws, derogates from the rules that normally govern the application of conflicting provisions of treaties, and provides that in the event that more than one regime might apply, the rule which shall prevail is neither the more recent nor the more specific, but instead that which is more favourable to the recognition and enforcement.

B. UNCITRAL Model Law on International Commercial Arbitration

The Model Law constitutes a sound basis for the desired harmonization and improvement of national laws. It covers all stages of the arbitral process from the arbitration agreement to the recognition and enforcement of the arbitral award and reflects a worldwide consensus on the principles and important issues of international arbitration practice. It is acceptable to states of all regions and the different legal or economic systems of the world. Since its adoption by UNCITRAL, the Model Law has come to represent the accepted international legislative standard for a modern arbitration law and a significant number of jurisdictions have enacted arbitration legislation based on the Model Law.

The principles and solutions adopted in the Model Law aim at reducing or eliminating the above-mentioned concerns and difficulties. As a response to the inadequacies and disparities of national laws, the Model Law presents a special legal regime tailored to international commercial arbitration, without affecting any relevant treaty in force in the state adopting the Model Law. While the Model Law was designed with international commercial arbitration in mind, it offers a set of basic rules that are not, in and of themselves, unsuitable to any other type of arbitration. States may thus consider extending their enactment of the Model Law to cover also domestic disputes, as a number of enacting states already have. In respect of the term "commercial", the Model Law provides no strict definition. The footnote to Article 1 (1) calls for "a wide interpretation" and offers an illustrative and open-ended list of relationships that might be described as commercial in nature, "whether contractual or not". The purpose of the footnote is to circumvent any technical difficulty that may arise, for example, in determining which transactions should be governed by a specific body of "commercial law" that may exist in some legal systems.

C. The 1961 European Convention on International Commercial Arbitration

The 1961 European Convention on International Commercial Arbitration is one of the two or three most important conventions in the area of International Commercial Arbitration. It provides a minimum set of standards for arbitration in signatory countries. Examples of important provisions in the Convention include those on: the procedures for appointing arbitrators when the parties cannot come to an agreement, the procedures for determining arbitral jurisdiction and applicable law when these have not been specified in the contract, and the right to appoint foreign arbitrators.

While some of these provisions also exist in internationally used arbitration rules, such as those of the International Chamber of Commerce (ICC) and the United Nations Commission on International Trade Law (UNCITRAL), or in the UNCITRAL Model Law for national legislation on international commercial arbitration, the 1961 European Convention remains the only place where they have been codified within an international legal instrument. This is important because it allows international commercial arbitration to be used, in a consistent manner, even under contracts where, for example, no specification is made of: the arbitration rules to be used, the applicable law and/or the place of arbitration. Some countries also find the 1961 European Convention useful because the conditions under which arbitration awards can be set aside are more restrictive than those found in the 1958 New York Convention on the Recognition and Enforcement of Foreign Arbitral Awards.

D. Inter-American Convention on International Commercial Arbitration

International commercial arbitration, and the cross-border recognition of arbitral decisions, has long been a subject of consideration between the Member States. In 1975 and 1979 they adopted two conventions in this area, the Inter-American Convention on International Commercial Arbitration (Panama Convention), and the Inter-American Convention on the Extraterritorial Validity of Foreign Judgments and Arbitral Awards (Montevideo Convention).

E. Inter-American Convention on Extraterritorial Validity of Foreign Judgments and Arbitral Awards

When one party to a dispute does not voluntarily comply with an arbitral decision, the success of international arbitration as a dispute resolution mechanism depends on local courts' correct application of legal principles to enforce it. This means that a country's legal system must: recognize the arbitration agreement, respond adequately to requests for preliminary injunctions and other precautionary measures to protect enforceability, in an avenue that ensure that successful claimant will actually recover the damages awarded it. Overall, the ability to enforce an arbitral judgment, and to do so through an expeditious process, are key aspects in any investor's risk assessments as he decides where he will invest capital, and in what amount. And the Montevideo Convention is made to guarantee the validity of the arbitral awards.

Exercise:

Please explain the function of commentary to international conventions.

Section 4 Sample Clause on Arbitration

In order to improve the efficiency, facilitate the parties and gain more competitive advantages, international arbitration institutions often provide some arbitration model clauses for the parties to choose. The design of these clauses also reflects the key points that need to be paid attention to when choosing arbitration as the method of dispute resolution, such as the place of arbitration, the selection of the applicable law, and the appointment of arbitrators.

A. ICC Model Arbitration Clause

International Chamber of Commerce (ICC) is the world business organization founded in 1919, representing business interests of companies and enabling business to secure peace, prosperity and opportunity for all. It also helps solve difficulties that arise in international commerce through the market leading administered dispute resolution services. Since 1923, the International Court of Arbitration has been helping to resolve difficulties in international commercial and business disputes to support trade and investment. Although it is called a court in name, it does not make formal judgments on disputed matters. Instead, the International Court of Arbitration exercises judicial supervision of arbitration proceedings. The model arbitration clauses are as follows:

"All disputes arising out of or in connection with the present contract shall be finally settled under the Rules of Arbitration of the International Chamber of Commerce by one or more arbitrators appointed in accordance with the said rules. Parties are free to adapt the clause to their particular circumstances. For instance, they may wish to stipulate the number of arbitrators, given that the ICC Arbitration Rules contain a presumption in favour of a sole arbitrator. Also, it may be desirable for them to stipulate the place and language of the arbitration and the law applicable to the merits. The ICC Arbitration Rules do not limit the parties' free choice of the place and language of the arbitration or the law governing the contract. When adapting the clause, care must be taken to avoid any risk of ambiguity. Unclear wording in the clause will cause uncertainty and delay and can hinder or even compromise the dispute resolution process. Parties should also take account of any factors that may affect the enforceability of the clause under the applicable law. These include any mandatory requirements that may exist at the place of arbitration and the expected place or places of enforcement."

B. SIAC Model Arbitration Clause

Established in 1991 as an independent, not-for-profit organization, Singapore International Arbitration (SIAC) has a proven track record in providing neutral arbitration services for the global business community. The centre is a company limited by guarantee established under the Company Law of the Republic of Singapore. SIAC specializes in resolving disputes in construction, shipping, banking, and insurance. Its purpose is to provide good services for international and domestic commercial arbitration and mediation, promote the wide application of arbitration and mediation in resolving commercial disputes, and train a group of arbitrators and experts who are familiar with international arbitration law and practice. Its arbitration rules are also maximally based on the UNCITRAL arbitration rules, with a great deal of autonomy for the parties.

"Any dispute arising out of or in connection with this contract, including any question regarding its existence, validity, or termination, shall be referred to and finally resolved by arbitration administered by the Singapore International Arbitration Centre ('SIAC') in accordance with the Arbitration Rules of the Singapore International Arbitration Centre ('SIAC Rules') for the time being in force, which rules are deemed to be incorporated by reference in this clause. The seat of the arbitration shall be [Singapore]***. The tribunal shall consist of *** arbitrator(s). The language of the arbitration shall be***."

C. SCC Model Arbitration Clause

The Arbitration Institute of the Stockholm Chamber of Commerce (SCC) was established in 1917 and is part of, but independent from, the Stockholm Chamber of Commerce. The SCC consists of a board and a secretariat and provides efficient dispute resolution services for both Swedish and international parties. Sweden and the SCC also play a unique role in the international system developed for bilateral and multilateral investment protection worldwide. Its arbitration model clauses are as follows:

"Any dispute, controversy or claim arising out of or in connection with this contract, or the breach, termination or invalidity thereof, shall be finally settled by arbitration in accordance with the Arbitration Rules of the Arbitration Institute of the Stockholm Chamber of Commerce." Recommended additions:

The arbitral tribunal shall be composed of three arbitrators/a sole arbitrator.

The seat of arbitration shall be [...].

The language of the arbitration shall be [...].

This contract shall be governed by the substantive law of [...].

D. HKIAC Model Arbitration Clause

The Hong Kong International Arbitration Centre (HKIAC) was established in 1985 by a group of leading businesspeople and professionals in an effort to meet the growing need for dispute resolution services in Asia. It is a company limited by guarantee and a non-profit organization established under Hong Kong law. Its arbitration model clauses are as follows:

Arbitration under the HKIAC Administered Arbitration Rules Parties to a contract who wish to have any future disputes referred to arbitration under the HKIAC Administered Arbitration Rules may insert in the contract an arbitration clause in the following form:

"Any dispute, controversy, difference or claim arising out of or relating to this contract, including the existence, validity, interpretation, performance, breach or termination thereof or any dispute regarding non-contractual obligations arising out of or relating to it shall be referred to and finally resolved by arbitration administered by the Hong Kong International Arbitration Centre (HKIAC) under the HKIAC Administered Arbitration Rules in force when the Notice of Arbitration is submitted.

The law of this arbitration clause shall be ... (Hong Kong law). ***

The seat of arbitration shall be ... (Hong Kong).

The number of arbitrators shall be ... (one or three). The arbitration proceedings shall be conducted in ... (insert language)."***

Parties to an existing dispute in which neither an arbitration clause nor a previous agreement with respect to arbitration exists, who wish to refer such dispute to arbitration under the HKIAC Administered Arbitration Rules, may agree to do so in the following terms:

We, the undersigned, agree to refer to arbitration administered by the Hong Kong International Arbitration Centre (HKIAC) under the HKIAC Administered Arbitration Rules any dispute, controversy, difference or claim (including any dispute regarding non-contractual obligations) arising out of or relating to: (Brief description of contract under which disputes, controversies, differences or claims have arisen or may arise).

The law of this arbitration agreement shall be ... (Hong Kong law).***

The seat of arbitration shall be ... (Hong Kong).

The number of arbitrators shall be ... (one or three). The arbitration proceedings shall be conducted in ... (insert language). ***

(1) Arbitration administered by HKIAC under the UNCITRAL Rules

"Any dispute, controversy, difference or claim arising out of or relating to this contract, including the existence, validity, interpretation, performance, breach or termination thereof or any dispute regarding non-contractual obligations arising out of or relating to it shall be referred to and finally resolved by arbitration administered by the Hong Kong International Arbitration Centre (HKIAC) under the UNCITRAL Arbitration Rules in force when the Notice of Arbitration is submitted, as modified by the HKIAC Procedures for the Administration of Arbitration under the UNCITRAL Arbitration Rules.

The law of this arbitration clause shall be ... (Hong Kong law).***

The place of arbitration shall be ... (Hong Kong).

The number of arbitrators shall be ... (one or three). The arbitration proceedings shall be conducted in ... (insert language)."***

(2) Ad hoc arbitration under the UNCITRAL Rules

"Any dispute, controversy, difference or claim arising out of or relating to this contract, including the existence, validity, interpretation, performance, breach or termination thereof or any dispute regarding non-contractual obligations arising out of or relating to it shall be referred to and finally resolved by arbitration under the UNCITRAL Arbitration Rules in force when the Notice of Arbitration is submitted.

The law of this arbitration clause shall be ... (Hong Kong law).***

The appointing authority shall be ... (Hong Kong International Arbitration Centre).

The place of arbitration shall be ... (Hong Kong).

The number of arbitrators shall be ... (one or three). The arbitration proceedings shall be conducted in ... (insert language)."***

(3) Domestic arbitration under the HKIAC Domestic Arbitration Rules

Parties to a contract who wish to have any future disputes referred to arbitration under the Domestic Arbitration Rules of the HKIAC may insert in the contract an arbitration clause in the following form: "Any dispute, controversy, difference or claim arising out of or relating to this contract, including the existence, validity, interpretation, performance, breach or termination thereof or any dispute regarding non-contractual obligations arising out of or relating to it shall be referred to and finally resolved by arbitration pursuant to the HKIAC Domestic Arbitration Rules in force when the Notice of Arbitration is submitted.

The law of this arbitration clause shall be ... (Hong Kong law).***

The seat of arbitration shall be ... (Hong Kong).

The number of arbitrators shall be ... (one or three). The arbitration proceedings shall be conducted in ... (insert language)."***

Parties to an existing dispute in which neither an arbitration clause nor a previous agreement with respect to arbitration exists, who wish to refer such dispute to arbitration under the HKIAC Domestic Arbitration Rules, may agree to do so in the following terms:

We, the undersigned, agree to refer to arbitration under the HKIAC Domestic Arbitration Rules in force when the Notice of Arbitration is submitted, any dispute, controversy, difference or claim (including any dispute regarding non-contractual obligations) arising out of or relating to: (Brief description of contract under which disputes, controversies, differences or claims have arisen or may arise).

The law of this arbitration agreement shall be ... (Hong Kong law). ***The seat of arbitration shall be ... (Hong Kong).

The number of arbitrators shall be ... (one or three). The arbitration proceedings shall be conducted in ... (insert language).***

E. CIETAC Model Arbitration Clause

The China International Economic and Trade Arbitration Commission (CIETAC) is one of the major permanent arbitration institutions in the world. CIETAC was set up in April 1956 under the China Council for the Promotion of International Trade (CCPIT) and renamed in 1980. It independently and impartially resolves economic and trade disputes, as well as investment disputes by means of arbitration. Headquartered in Beijing, CIETAC has several sub-commissions in other cities of China. Its arbitration model clauses are as follows:

Any dispute arising from or in connection with this contract shall be submitted to China International Economic and Trade Arbitration Commission (CIETA) for arbitration which shall be conducted in accordance with the CIETAC's arbitration rules in effect at the time of applying for arbitration. The arbitral award is final and binding upon both parties.

Any dispute arising from or in connection with this Contract shall be submitted to China International Economic and Trade Arbitration Commission (CIETAC)*** Sub-Commission (Arbitration Center) for arbitration which shall be conducted in accordance with the CIETAC's arbitration rules in effect at the time of applying for arbitration. The arbitral award is final and binding upon both parties.

F. AAA Model Arbitration Clause

The not-for-profit American Arbitration Association (AAA) International Centre for Dispute Resolution (ICDR) is the largest private global provider of alternative dispute resolution (ADR) services in the world. Founded in 1926, the American Arbitration Association is headquartered in New York City and has 34 offices in the United States, as well as two international centers in New York and Dublin. It provides the arbitration model clause as follows:

Any controversy or claim arising out of or relating to this contract, or the breach thereof, shall be settled by arbitration administered by the American Arbitration Association under its Commercial Arbitration Rules, and judgment on the award rendered by the arbitrator(s) may be entered in any court having jurisdiction thereof.

Exercise:

Please share initial thoughts on comparing sample arbitration clauses from various arbitration institutions.

Section 5　Chinese Arbitration Law

A. Arbitration Law of the People's Republic of China (2017 Amendment)

1. "Arbitration commission"

Article 11   An arbitration commission shall meet the conditions set forth below:

(1) To have its own name, domicile and charter;

(2) To have the necessary property;

(3) To have the personnel that are to form the commission; and

(4) To have appointed arbitrators.

The charter of an arbitration commission shall be formulated in accordance with this law.

2. "China Arbitration Association"

Article 15   China Arbitration Association is a social organization with the status of a legal person. Arbitration commissions are members of China Arbitration Association. The charter of China Arbitration Association shall be formulated by its national congress of members.

China Arbitration Association is a self-disciplined organization of arbitration commissions. It shall, in accordance with its charter, supervise arbitration commissions and their members and arbitrators as to whether or not they breach discipline.

China Arbitration Association shall formulate rules of arbitration in accordance with this law and the relevant provisions of the Civil Procedure Law.

3. "Arbitration agreement"

An arbitration agreement shall include arbitration clauses stipulated in the contract and agreements of submission to arbitration that are concluded in other written forms before or after disputes arise.

An arbitration agreement shall contain the following particulars:

(1) an expression of intention to apply for arbitration;

(2) matters for arbitration; and

(3) a designated arbitration commission.

B. Chinese Judicial Interpretations

1. Interpretation of the Supreme People's Court concerning Some Issues on Application of the Arbitration Law of the People's Republic of China

(1) "Agreements for arbitration in other written forms"

Article 1   The term "agreements for arbitration in other written forms" as prescribed in Article 16 of the Arbitration Law shall include the agreements on resorting to arbitration which are reached in the forms of contracts, letters or data message (including telegraph, telefax, fax, electronic data interchange and e-mail), etc.

(2) "The first hearing"

Article 14   The term "the first hearing" as mentioned in Article 26 of the Arbitration

Law shall refer to the first trial in court, which is organized by the people's court after expiry of the period for defense, excluding all procedural activities prior to the trial.

(3) "No agreement for arbitration"

The term "no agreement for arbitration" as prescribed in Item (1) of 229 Paragraph 1 of Article 58 of the Arbitration Law shall refer to that the parties concerned did not reach an agreement for arbitration. If the agreement for arbitration is ascertained as ineffective or is revoked, it shall be deemed that there is no agreement for arbitration.

(4) "Violation of legal procedures"

Article 20　The term "violation of legal procedures" as prescribed in Article 58 of the Arbitration Law shall refer to violation of the arbitration procedures prescribed in the Arbitration Law or a circumstance under which the arbitration rules chosen by the parties concerned might affect the correct award for the case.

C. Arrangement Concerning Mutual Assistance in Court-ordered Interim Measures in Aid of Arbitral Proceedings by the Courts of the Mainland and of the Hong Kong Special Administrative Region

1. "Interim measure"

Article 1　"Interim measure" referred to in this arrangement includes, in the case of the Mainland, property preservation, evidence preservation and conduct preservation; and, in the case of the HKSAR, injunction and other interim measures for the purpose of maintaining or restoring the status quo pending determination of the dispute; taking action that would prevent, or refraining from taking action that is likely to cause current or imminent harm or prejudice to the arbitral proceedings; preserving assets; or preserving evidence that may be relevant and material to the resolution of the dispute.

2. "Arbitral proceedings in Hong Kong"

Article 2　"Arbitral proceedings in Hong Kong" referred to in this arrangement shall be seated in the HKSAR and be administered by the following institutions or permanent offices:

(1) arbitral institutions established in the HKSAR or having their headquarters established in the HKSAR, and with their principal place of management located in the HKSAR;

(2) dispute resolution institutions or permanent offices set up in the HKSAR by international intergovernmental organizations of which the People's Republic of China is a member; or

(3) dispute resolution institutions or permanent offices set up in the HKSAR by other arbitral institutions and which satisfy the criteria prescribed by the HKSAR Government (such as the number of arbitration cases and the amount in dispute, etc.). The list of such institutions or permanent offices referred to above is to be provided by the HKSAR Government to the Supreme People's Court and be subject to confirmation by both sides.

3. Provisions of the Supreme People's Court on Several Issues concerning the Handling of Cases regarding Enforcement of Arbitral Awards by the People's Courts

"cases regarding enforcement of arbitral awards"

Article 1　The term "cases regarding enforcement of arbitral awards" as mentioned in these provisions refers to cases where a party files an application with the people's court for enforcement of an arbitral award or a written arbitral mediation rendered by an arbitral institution in accordance with the Arbitration Law.

Arbitration is an internationally accepted method of dispute settlement and an important part of China's alternative dispute resolution mechanism. It plays an irreplaceable role in protecting the legitimate rights and interests of the parties, ensuring healthy economic development and promoting international economic exchanges. China's current Arbitration Law was promulgated in 1994, and certain provisions were amended in 2009 and 2017 respectively. Since its implementation 26 years ago, the Arbitration Law has played a positive and important role. However, the Arbitration Law has also revealed some problems that do not adapt to the new development of the situation and the needs of arbitration practice in these yeas. The Ministry of Justice issued the Arbitration Law of the People's Republic of China (Revised) (Draft for Comments) and its explanations in July 2021 to solicit public opinions, aiming at improving the arbitration system and enhancing the credibility of arbitration.

Exercises:

1. Please explain the system of Chinese arbitration law.
2. Please explain key elements in judging an effective arbitration agreement.

Chapter 10
Dispute Resolution-Mediation

调解是一种灵活的争议解决方式，它以中立的方式帮助双方通过谈判解决争议。双方对和解的决定和任何协议的条款都有控制权。成功的调解会产生对当事人有合同约束力的协议。如果一方当事人不尊重和解协议，另一方当事人可以寻求法院强制执行和解协议。由于调解能让各方更好地了解彼此的业务需求，明确争议焦点，缓解双方对抗的压力，容易寻求到双赢的解决方案，维护后续长期的合作关系，越来越多的争议当事方选择调解作为争议解决方式。《新加坡调解公约》的出现适应了调解快速发展的趋势，也推动着调解这一纠纷解决机制的完善与普及。各大争端解决机构往往也会为当事人提供比较灵活和自由的调解服务。

本章将从不同角度解释调解的含义，介绍与调解有关的具有影响力的国际公约及其报告，以加深读者对调解的理解。也介绍了部分仲裁机构制定的调解示范条款，可适用于不同类型的纠纷，其中包括了与仲裁程序的选择、衔接与适用等内容。此外，本章还介绍了中国法律制度下常见的几种调解形式以及调解实践中的相关规则。

Section 1 Definition of Mediation

A. Definition from Law Dictionaries

Different legal dictionaries have different perceptions of mediation. *Black's Law Dictionary* sees mediation as a method of non-binding dispute resolution involving a neutral third party who tries to help the disputing parties reach a mutually agreeable solution.

English-Chinese Dictionary of Anglo-American Law considers mediation as a dispute resolution process by a neutral third party, the conciliator, in private and informal capacity, to assist the parties to a dispute in reaching a settlement.

In contrast, the definitions of mediation in *The Oxford Companion to Law* and *The Longman Dictionary of Law* are much shorter.

The former considers mediation to be the intervention of a third party attempting to resolve a conflict between two others, while the latter considers mediation to be the act of a neutral third party relating to the settling of a dispute between two contending parties.

B. Definition from Leading Scholars

Christopher Moore holds mediation is a conflict resolution process in which a mutually acceptable third party, who has no authority to make binding decisions for disputants, intervenes in a conflict or dispute to assist the parties in improving their relationships, enhance communications, and use effective problem-solving and negotiation procedures to reach voluntary and mutually acceptable understandings or agreements on contested issues. The procedure is an extension of the negotiation process. Mediation is commonly initiated when disputing parties on their own are not able to start productive talks or have initiated discussions and reached an impasse.

Jay Folberg and Alison Taylor say mediation is an alternative to violence, self-help, or litigation that differs from the processes of counseling, negotiation, and arbitration. It can be defined as the process by which the participants, together with the assistance of a neutral person or persons, systematically isolate disputed issues in order to develop options, consider alternatives and reach a consensual settlement that will accommodate their needs. Mediation is a process that emphasizes the participants' own responsibility for making decisions that affect their lives. It is therefore a self-empowering process.

Laurence Boulle and Miryana Nesic's views are somewhat similar to those of the first two scholars. They argue that mediation is a decision-making process in which the parties are assisted by a third party, the mediator attempts to improve the process of decision-making and to assist the parties in reaching an outcome to which each of them can assent.

Exercises:

1. Please summarize key elements in defining mediation.
2. Please explain the advantages of mediation compared with other dispute resolution methods.

Section 2 International Convention

A. The United Nations Convention on International Settlement Agreements Resulting from Mediation (2018)

This Convention is an instrument for the facilitation of international trade and the promotion of mediation as an alternative and effective method of resolving trade disputes. Being a binding international instrument, it is expected to bring certainty and stability to the international framework on mediation. The United Nations Convention on International Settlement Agreements Resulting from Mediation (Singapore Convention on Mediation) states that mediation means a process, irrespective of the expression used or the basis upon which the process is carried out, whereby parties attempt to reach an amicable settlement of their dispute with the assistance of a third person or persons ("the mediator") lacking the authority to impose a solution upon the parties to the dispute. The Convention applies to international settlement agreements resulting from mediation, concluded in writing by parties to resolve a commercial dispute. It also lists the exclusions from the scope of the Convention, namely, settlement agreements concluded by a consumer for personal, family or household purposes, or relating to family, inheritance or employment law. The Convention is consistent with the UNCITRAL Model Law on International Commercial Mediation and International Settlement Agreements resulting from Mediation (2018). This approach is intended to provide States with the flexibility to adopt either the Convention, the Model Law as a standalone text or both the Convention and the Model Law as complementary instruments of a comprehensive legal framework on mediation.

B. UNCITRAL Model Law on International Commercial Mediation and International Settlement Agreements Resulting from Mediation (2018)

The Model Law was initially adopted in 2002. It was known as the "Model Law on International Commercial Conciliation", and it covered the conciliation procedure. The Model Law has been amended in 2018 with the addition of a new section on international settlement agreements and their enforcement. The Model Law has been renamed "Model Law on International Commercial Mediation and International Settlement Agreements Resulting from Mediation". In its previously adopted texts and relevant documents, UNCITRAL used the term "conciliation" with the understanding that the terms "conciliation" and "mediation" were interchangeable.

The term "conciliation" is used throughout the UNCITRAL Model Law on International Commercial Conciliation (2002). Conciliation means a process, whether referred to by the expression conciliation, mediation or an expression of similar import, whereby parties request a third person or persons ("the conciliator") to assist them in their attempt to reach an amicable settlement of their dispute arising out of or relating to a contractual or other legal relationship. The conciliator does not have the authority to impose upon the parties a solution to the dispute. In amending the Model Law, UNCITRAL decided to use the term "mediation" instead in an effort to adapt to the actual and practical use of the terms and with the expectation that this change will facilitate the promotion and heighten the visibility of the Model Law. This change in terminology does not have any substantive or conceptual implications.

To avoid uncertainty resulting from an absence of statutory provisions, the Model Law addresses procedural aspects of mediation, including appointment of conciliators, commencement and termination of mediation, conduct of the mediation, communication between the mediator and other parties, confidentiality and admissibility of evidence in other proceedings as well as post-mediation issues, such as the mediator acting as arbitrator and enforceability of settlement agreements. The Model Law provides uniform rules on enforcement of settlement agreements and also addresses the right of a party to invoke a settlement agreement in a procedure. It provides an exhaustive list of grounds that a party can invoke in a procedure covered by the Model Law.

C. WIPO Alternative Dispute Resolution

World Intellectual Property Organization (WIPO) is the global forum for intellectual property (IP) services, policy, information and cooperation. It is a self-funding agency of the United Nations to lead the development of a balanced and effective international IP system that enables innovation and creativity for the benefit of all. Its mandate, governing bodies and procedures are set out in the WIPO Convention, which established WIPO in 1967. WIPO also provides the alternative dispute resolution services, such as mediation and expert determination to enable private parties to settle their domestic or cross-border commercial disputes.

Guide to WIPO Mediation holds that mediation is an informal consensual process in which a neutral intermediary, the mediator, assists the parties in reaching a settlement of their dispute, based on the parties' respective interests. Mediation is an efficient and cost-effective way of achieving that result while preserving, and at times even enhancing, the relationship of the parties. Guide to WIPO Mediation also emphasizes that mediation is a non-binding procedure controlled by the parties. A party to a mediation cannot be forced to accept an outcome that it does not like. The mediator is not a decision-maker, but to assist the parties in reaching a settlement of the dispute.

D. Perspective of the Practice

From the perspective of the practice, the Hong Kong International Arbitration Centre

Mediation Rules define mediation as a confidential, voluntary, non-binding and private dispute resolution process in which a neutral person (the mediator) helps the parties to reach a negotiated settlement. Influenced by this, the Hong Kong Mediation Centre Mediation Rules consider mediation to be a structured confidential, voluntary and private dispute resolution process comprising one or more sessions in which one or more impartial individuals (the mediator), without adjudicating a dispute or and aspect of it, assists the parties to the dispute in reaching a negotiated settlement.

ICC considers that mediation is a flexible and consensual technique in which a neutral facility helps the parties reach a negotiated settlement of their dispute. The parties have control over the decision to settle and the terms of any agreement. Settlements are contractually binding and widely enforceable. All ICC Mediations are administered by the ICC International Centre for ADR and follow the ICC Mediation Rules.

Singapore International Mediation Centre (SIMC) considers that the non-adversarial and flexible nature of mediation saves time and cost, particularly in cross-border cases which may involve instructing counsel from multiple jurisdictions as well as complex conflicts of law issues. Since the mediator does not adjudicate on the dispute, parties have full control over the outcome of the dispute. They can agree on legal and non-legal solutions that are forward-looking and suited to their interests and needs. In the event of a non-settlement, the process of mediation often brings added clarity to the scope and nature of the dispute. Mediation at SIMC also comes with the unique benefit of enforceability: Settlement agreements may be made consent awards under an Arb-Med-Arb Protocol between the Singapore International Arbitration Centre (SIAC) and SIMC.

In the U.S. Uniform Mediation Act, mediation means a process in which a mediator facilitates communication and negotiation between parties to assist them in reaching a voluntary agreement regarding their dispute.

If mediation is successful, parties will enter into a settlement agreement, which can be enforced under the Singapore Mediation Act. With the deposit of the third instrument of ratification, the Singapore Convention on Mediation has entered into force on September 12, 2020. This essentially allows for international mediated settlement agreements to be enforced or invoked in a signatory jurisdiction.

Exercise:

Please explain the innovation of Singapore Convention on Mediation.

Section 3 Commentary/ Explanation Report

In the UNCITRAL Model Law on International Commercial Mediation and International Settlement Agreements Resulting from Mediation, mediation means a process, whether referred to by the expression mediation, conciliation or an expression of similar import, whereby parties request a third person or persons ("the mediator") to assist them in their attempt in reaching an amicable settlement of their dispute arising out of or relating to a contractual or other legal relationship. The mediator does not have the authority to impose upon the parties a solution to the dispute.

Exercise:
Please evaluate the influence of Model Law in the area of dispute resolution.

Section 4 Sample Clauses on Mediation

Mediation organizations tend to provide the parties with sample clauses about mediation in advance. These sample clauses can be long or short and vary in content.

A. CCPIT/CCOIC Sample Mediation Clause

Founded in 1952, China Council for the Promotion of International Trade (CCPIT) is a national foreign trade and investment promotion agency. Affiliated to China Council for the CCPIT, CCOIC is a nationwide chamber of commerce comprised of enterprises, groups and other business organizations that are engaged in international commercial activities in China.

On the official website of the CCPIT/CCOIC Mediation Center, the Center provides its sample clause: The parties hereto are willing to submit any dispute arising out of or in connection with this contract to the CCPIT/CCOIC Mediation Center for mediation in accordance with the mediation rules in effect at the time of the application for mediation. If a settlement agreement is reached after mediation, each party shall perform in good faith all the elements contained in such settlement agreement.

B. SIMC Sample Mediation Clause

The Singapore International Mediation Centre (SIMC) is an independent, not-for-profit organization dedicated to meeting the evolving business needs of Asia. SIMC was established on 5 November 2014 following the recommendations of a Working Group convened by Chief Justice Sundaresh Menon and the Ministry of Law, on developing Singapore into a hub for international commercial mediation.

SIMC Mediation Clause distinguish between the different stages at which a dispute arises. The details are as follows.

"For use before a dispute arises:

All disputes, controversies or differences arising out of or in connection with this contract, including any question regarding its existence, validity or termination, shall be first referred to mediation in Singapore in accordance with the Mediation Rules of the Singapore International Mediation Centre for the time being in force.

For use after a dispute has arisen:

All disputes, controversies or differences arising out of or in connection with this contract, including any question regarding its existence, validity or termination, notwithstanding the commencement of any other proceedings, shall be referred to mediation in Singapore in accordance with the Mediation Rules of the Singapore International Mediation Centre for the time being in force."

C. SCC Sample Mediation Clause

The SCC model clauses are more complex and detailed, consisting of three parts. The original article is as follows.

1. "Model Mediation Clause"

Any dispute, controversy or claim arising out of or in connection with this contract, or the breach, termination or invalidity thereof, shall be referred to mediation in accordance with the Mediation Rules of the Arbitration Institute of the Stockholm Chamber of Commerce, unless one of the parties objects.

2. "Combined Clause"

Any dispute, controversy or claim arising out of or in connection with this contract, or the breach, termination or invalidity thereof, shall first be referred to Mediation in accordance with the Mediation Rules of the Arbitration Institute of the Stockholm Chamber of Commerce, unless one of the parties' objects.

If one of the parties objects to Mediation or if the Mediation is terminated, the dispute shall be finally resolved ...

IMPORTANT:

When using the model clause, one of the options below should be inserted.

Option 1

... by arbitration in accordance with the Arbitration Rules of the Arbitration Institute of the Stockholm Chamber of Commerce.

Option 2

... by arbitration in accordance with the Rules for Expedited Arbitrations of the Arbitration Institute of the Stockholm Chamber of Commerce.

Option 3

... by arbitration at the Arbitration Institute of the Stockholm Chamber of Commerce (the SCC).

The Rules for Expedited Arbitrations shall apply, unless the SCC, taking into account the complexity of the case, the amount in dispute and other circumstances, determines that the Arbitration Rules of the Arbitration Institute of the Stockholm Chamber of Commerce shall apply. In the latter case, the SCC shall also decide whether the tribunal shall be composed of one or three arbitrators.

Option 4

... in any court of competent jurisdiction."

D. LCIA Sample Mediation Clause

The London Court of International Arbitration (LCIA) is a not-for-profit company limited by guarantee. The LCIA provides flexible administration of arbitration and of a wide range of other ADR procedures, regardless of the location of the parties, and under any system of law.

LCIA Recommended Clauses cover three specific situations: "Mediation only", "Arbitration only" and "Mediation and Arbitration".

1. "Mediation only"

'In the event of a dispute arising out of or relating to this contract, including any question regarding its existence, validity or termination, the parties shall seek settlement of that dispute by mediation in accordance with the LCIA Mediation Rules, which rules are deemed to be incorporated by reference into this clause.'

2. "Arbitration only"

'Any dispute arising out of or in connection with this contract, including any question regarding its existence, validity or termination, shall be referred to and finally resolved by arbitration under the Rules of the LCIA, which rules are deemed to be incorporated by reference into this clause.

The number of arbitrators shall be [one/three].

The seat, or legal place, of arbitration shall be [City and/or Country].

The language to be used in the arbitration shall be [...].

The governing law of the contract shall be the substantive law of [...].'

3. "Mediation and Arbitration"

'In the event of a dispute arising out of or relating to this contract, including any question regarding its existence, validity or termination, the parties shall first seek settlement of that dispute by mediation in accordance with the LCIA Mediation Rules, which Rules are deemed to be incorporated by reference into this clause.

If the dispute is not settled by mediation within [...] days of the commencement of the mediation, or such further period as the parties shall agree in writing, the dispute shall be referred to and finally resolved by arbitration under the LCIA Rules, which rules are deemed to be incorporated by reference into this clause.

The language to be used in the mediation and in the arbitration shall be [...].

The governing law of the contract shall be the substantive law of [...].

In any arbitration commenced pursuant to this clause,

(i) the number of arbitrators shall be [one/three]; and

(ii) the seat, or legal place, of arbitration shall be [City and/or Country].'

Exercise:

Please compare differences of sample clauses on mediation as well as those on arbitration.

Section 5　Chinese Mediation Law

In China, mediation mainly takes the following forms: litigation mediation, administrative mediation, arbitration mediation and people's mediation. There are few laws on commercial mediation.

A. Litigation Mediation

For litigation mediation, the people's court facilitates the parties to reach an agreement to end the litigation by means of legal education and guidance. The people's court must conduct conciliation on the basis of voluntary action by both parties. If the parties refuse conciliation, the people's court cannot force the parties to accept conciliation. The mediation agreement must be reached voluntarily by both parties with mutual understanding and accommodation. According to the provisions of the Civil Procedure Law, mediation should ascertain the facts and distinguish right from wrong.

B. People's Mediation

People's mediation is a form of mediation outside the litigation as recognized in Chinese law. It has its own unique organizational form, complete working principles, systems, procedures, strict work discipline, convenient and flexible, diversified work methods. The People's Mediation Law provides that the term "people's mediation" refers to a process that a people's mediation commission persuades the parties concerned to a dispute to reach a mediation agreement on the basis of equal negotiation and free will and thus solves the dispute between them. The civil disputes mediated by the people's mediation committees include all kinds of disputes involving civil rights and obligations between citizens and citizens, citizens and legal persons, and other social organizations.

For reference, the Mediation Rules of Shanghai Commercial Mediation Center (For Trial Implementation) hold that mediation means a process, applied by the applicant or entrusted by another agency, whereby parties attempt to reach an amicable settlement of their dispute with the assistance of a third person or persons ("the mediator") who facilitates the parties to the dispute to arrive at a mutually acceptable solution.

Exercises:
1. Please explain the system of Chinese Mediation Law.
2. Explain the functions of Mediation Rules in practice.

Chapter 11
Writing Basics

本章介绍了法律英语写作的基本流程和步骤，以及在起草法律文书时应注意的一些重要问题。遵循常用的方法或格式，有助于厘清写作思路，使实际起草过程更容易。写作的基本过程首先需明确该次写作需实现何种目的，目标读者是谁，读者的要求是什么，从而才能明确写作需呈现的内容重点与语言风格。在正式动笔前列出详细的大纲，能够有条理地展现思路及整体结构。写作结束后还需对内容及格式进行检查和修订，这样才能算真正地完成写作。

具体到写作方式上，本章从用词、语言风格、句法及标点符号的使用方面进行展开。在用词方面，法律文书写作需使用具体的、准确的、专业的及简洁的语言。其中包括动词与名词的选择、对时间及期限的描述、连词的准确使用等。在语言风格方面，法律专业写作中写文件的语气要正式，应避免口语化的表述。在句子使用方面，我们要注意长短句的使用及逻辑的正确表达，避免出现语法错误、内容缺失等问题。

Writing involves planning—the more planning, the more effective the written document. Legal writing has three components: prewriting, drafting and revising. The key to effective writing includes clarity and organization.

Section 1　Writing Process

Follow a method or format when preparing to write to make the actual drafting process easier. The fundamental components of process writing are assessing the document's purpose and intended audience, drafting a detailed outline before writing, revising your findings into the categories of purpose and audience, and outlining and revising your work.

A. Prepare to Write: Purpose and Audience

Determine the purpose of the document, and find out who the readers will be. First, to determine the consultation document needs to solve legal questions. The writers need to understand the requirements of the clients or readers. For example, on which aspects of the contents of this writing involved need to be explained emphatically from the parties, which aspects need only simple instructions and which matters need the readers to reach a consensus.

The readers may concern for the related law but they do not understand, they may also lack legal knowledge experience to deal with problems. The readers may only tell what difficulties they have, so the writer needs to find out the specific problems and understand the requirements.

Second, the writers need to determine the main audience, consulting documents and understand its background, including legal knowledge background and business background. For example, issuing a consultation paper about an investment project, the writer needs to consider whether the parties will show the writing to the partner lawyer, investor, or investor's lawyer. A lawyer of the readers when reading a document would prefer to read about the law and legal analysis of the problems, and documents need to be more professional. And for the ordinary reader, it is better to write in an easier way. For example, a business person may know little about law and legal analysis, he would want to know about their business risks or economic loss. Therefore, the legal writing needs to be easy for the audience and respond to his concerns.

B. Drafting a Detailed Outline

Outlie the issues, assertions or points that you want to include.

First, to determine the structure of the instrument. Again, there is no stereotyped best structure for the legal writing. In the chart below is a list of two kinds of basic structure. In the actual operation process, the writer needs to consider the actual situation of the parties and the case for the structure adjustment, or adopt other new structures.

First Structure
Facts
Facing problems
Relevant laws and regulations
The application of law to the facts
Conclusion

(To be continued)

Second Structure
Question presented
A general answer
Laws and regulations of the relevant facts and assumptions
The application of law to the facts
Conclusion

Formulating outline helps writer to dispose materials that has been collected before. According to the actual situation of the case, the writer needs to modify the legal writing of the precedent text (if any).

C. Revision: The Final Part of the Process

After modifying, it is necessary for the writer to do a final check before sending the documents to the customer: (1) to ensure that the recipient's name is written correctly; (2) to review the purpose, the audience of the intended document, and check the outline for appropriateness; (3) to ensure that the mentioned attachment is attached after documents and sent to the readers; (4) to ensure the correct character, grammar, and punctuation.

D. Example of Process Writing Techniques

Ms. Partner calls you into her office and asks you to prepare a client letter to Mrs. Jones, advising her as to a course of action that she can take to rectify the problem of her mislabeled fur coat. The facts of the problem are as follows:

Mrs. Jones bought a fur coat from John J. Furriers. The coat was labeled 100 percent raccoon. One day, Mrs. Jones was smoking a cigarette and a hot ash fell on the coat while she was wearing it. The ash melted a hole in the coat. Mrs. Jones knew that fur burns, but acrylic melts.

Consider all the process of writing, and revise all your prewriting steps by checking your purpose, audience and outline once again. Now you are ready to write.

Exercises:

Based on Example of Process Writing Techniques, please list the points you would like to address in the letter.

References:

a. The fur coat was mislabeled.

b. The seller misrepresented his product.

c. *If the misrepresentation was intentional, there is possibility of fraud.*

d. *Mrs. Jones would like to obtain a full refund for the coat that she purchased.*

e. *If a refund is not given in seven days, court action will proceed.*

Section 2　Clear Writing and Editing

Preparing a first draft of a document can be quite an undertaking, but that is only a start. You have not completed your project until you have carefully edited and revised your drafts at least once.

A. Diction

Diction means choice of words when writing.

Selecting the appropriate words to express your idea is a skill that is developed over time.

1. Select concrete words

In general, selecting concrete words allows the readers to visualize what you are saying. It makes the legal writing more readable and effective.

(1) Use less abstract words

Abstract words describe the abstract ideas or general concepts, such as "justice" and "device". Concrete words express the details and tangible items, such as "court" and "car". Read the following examples:

He harmed one of his body parts in the device at issue in the case.

His arm was severed when the threshing machine stalled and he fell forward in front of the machine.

The second example is clear because the reader knows what happened to the body part. Certainly, if the writing aims to avoid the adverse impacts of your customer, there is no need to use concrete words to describe details.

(2) Use more verbs

Generally, the verbs can exactly describe how the action takes than nouns. When a noun has a verb form, it is better to use the verb form and avoid the noun form to describe the action.

Read the following examples:

a. *The parties entered into an agreement on July 8, 2012.*

b. *There was an agreement entered into on July 8, 2012.*

c. *The parties agreed to the terms on July 8, 2012.*

The last example is the best because it is the simplest and it uses the word "agreed" as a verb rather than as a noun. It is the easiest sentence of the three to understand and to visualize. Meanwhile, it is better to use the completely written form and avoid using the abbreviated form of verbs, such as "don't", "doesn't".

More verbs as follows:

with the intention to—intend to

in representation of—represent

bring about a resolution—resolve

make a determination—determine

make an assumption—assume

make a proposition or proposal—propose

take sth into consideration—consider

state by implication—imply

reach an agreement—agree

2. Select accurate words

The words showing the exact meaning is important in legal writing. Small confusion may cause serious consequence.

a. Use accurate words to describe date and period

Time and period are very important in legal issue, such as the repayment date and length of maturity. However, the parties often ignore the period until the deadline approached. The calculations in period and time are often decisive, which usually causes the disputes between parties. When describing date or period, it needs to write clearly.

Read the following examples:

Alice shall pay 200$ to Bob in a week.

Alice shall pay 200$ to Bob in 7 calendar days, and the signing day is not counted.

For the first sentence, whether a "week" means 7 calendar days or 5 workdays is not clear. Whether the period contains the signing day is also not accurate. The second sentence uses the accurate words to express clearly.

"Week" usually have three main meanings: (1) seven-day cycles used in various calendars; (2) any seven consecutive days; (3) the normal workday or school day of each seven-day cycle. Therefore, when using the word "week" to describe a period, we must be very careful to clarify the exact days.

Similarly, just using the word "month" to describe the period is also easy to cause ambiguity. Therefore, it needs to clarify the starting date and the number of days.

As for "day", it is necessary to clarify whether it is a calendar day or work day and how to determine the business day at certain location.

Another point of confusion is the calculation of time span. Read the following example:

The party shall exercise the option within 30 days and notify the other party immediately.

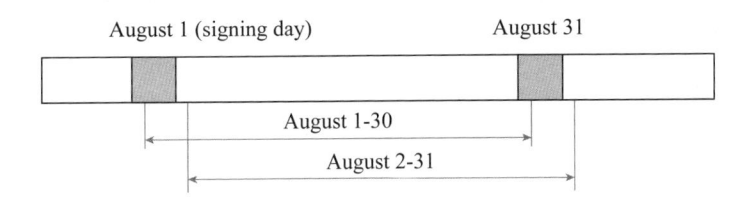

```
         August 1 (signing day)          August 31
         |                                  |
         └──────── August 1-30 ─────────────┘
              └──── August 2-31 ────────────┘
```

"Within 30 days" may have two calculation periods. One is from August 1 to August 30, which started from the signing day. Another one is from August 2 to August 31, which did not include the signing day. If the period is not certain enough, the disputes will raise when the deadline comes.

The Civil Code of the People's Republic of China has ruled the time periods as follows:

Article 200　For the purpose of the Civil Law, a time period shall be calculated by the Gregorian calendar in years, months, days and hours.

Article 201　When a time period is calculated in years, months, and days, the day on which the period begins shall not be counted as within the period; calculation shall begin from the next day.

When a time period is calculated in hours, the calculation of such a period shall begin from the time stipulated by the law or agreed by the parties concerned.

Article 202　When a time period is calculated in years and months, the same day of the last month as the day on which the period begins shall be taken as the last day of the time period; where there is no such a day, the end of the last month shall be taken as the last day of the time period.

Article 203　If the last day of a time period falls on a Sunday or an official holiday, the day after the holiday shall be taken as the last day of the time period.

The last day of a time period shall end at 24:00. If business hours are applicable, the last day shall end at the closing time for business.

b. Use "and" "or" accurately

When choosing words with accurate meaning, the word "and" needs to be carefully considered.

Read the following examples:

Mary and David will inherit 80,000$.

Which one is the true meaning of this sentence:

(1) Mary and David, the two persons together, shared 80,000$ jointly.

(2) Mary will inherit 80,000$. David will inherit 80,000$. Each of them can acquire 80,000$.

Read other examples:

The stud-farm shall deliver all the black and white horses to the designated place agreed in contract.

However, there are pure white horses, pure black horses, and black and white zebras in the stud-farm. What kind of horse are the clause required?

"And" has several meanings:

(1) severally: white and black horse then refers to all white horses, and all black horses.

(2) jointly: white and black horse then refers to a horse that is both white and black.

(3) combine severally and jointly: white and black horse then refers to pure white horses, pure black horses, and the mixed-color black and white horses.

It is a good way to clarify the exact meaning of "and" by adding details like "severally", "jointly", "both" or "each" and relative clauses.

Read the following example:

The new regulation will be applied in Shanghai or Jiangsu from September 1st, 2022.

Which one is the true meaning of the above-mentioned example:

The new regulation will be applied in Shanghai, or in Jiangsu, but not in both.

The new regulation will be applied in Shanghai, or in Jiangsu, or in both.

"Or" has two common meanings: for the first sentence, "or" refers to exclusive meaning; for the second sentence, "or" refers to inclusive meaning. Therefore, it is better to write clearly when using this word.

c. Use modal verbs accurately

In legal writing, the function of modal verbs is to modify certain clauses and make them reflect the writer's correct judgment on the meaning of the clauses or reflect our own judgments about the content. The modals show a range of different meanings: permission, obligation, and determination. All is related to people's ability to control events. At the same time, modal verbs also express the meaning of "possible", "must" and "expected", which is the judgment of possible events. The following is a brief introduction to the main usages of the four modal verbs.

(1) Shall: usually describe obligation or duty

The meaning of "shall" is slightly different from the word "will". In oral English, we usually use the word "will" to express obligation. For example:

If I break the contract, I will pay the contract liquidated damages.

However, it is more common and more accurate to use "shall" to express obligation in legal documents. For example:

(1) The breaching party shall pay liquidated damages to the other party.

(2) If one party is unable to perform the contract due to force majeure, it shall notify the other party in time.

(2) Must: usually describe obligation or duty

For example:

Party A must provide the goods of qualified quality as agreed in the contract.

It should be noted that use "shall" or "must" consistently. If you choose to use "must" to describe obligation first, you also need to use "must" in the following writing.

(3) May: describe the permission or discretion or the possibility

The word "may" has the same meaning as the word "shall" to express obligation. This is the important factor that can easily cause ambiguity and disputes. Clarifying the specific meaning of "may" needs to be interpreted according to the context or even the purpose of the document. Therefore, in order to avoid controversy, it is better to use "shall" to describe obligation and use "may" to describe option when writing.

(4) Will: describe the future

For example:

Party A will deliver the product to Party B before September 3rd, 2022.

The writers need remember to choose the most appropriate modals for the situation so that the writing can express the accurate meaning.

Other usages of modal verbs are as follows:

is obligated—shall/must

undertakes to—shall/must

covenants to—shall/must

is responsible to—shall/must

is authorized to—may

is entitled to—may

have the option to—may

be free to—may

have the discretion to—may

3. Select professional words

For legal writing, professional terms usually have special meaning in the legal area which are different from the common meaning. There are also some certain words or collocations that are established practice in legal writing. Select professional words to show professionalism.

Read the following examples:

Compare the meaning of "bench".

(1) Each bench will seat four persons.

(2) This dispute was settled by bench trial.

Compare the use of words:

(1) The contracting party is exempted due to earthquake, hurricane and other similar accidents.

(2) The contracting party is exempted due to force majeure, including but not limited to earthquake and hurricane.

The second sentence is more professional because it is the legal term used in legal writing. The word contains specific meaning and interpretation which is also more accurate and concise.

Some professional words are common in plain English, such as the lawyer, individual, contract, trial, debt, crime and so on. These words are not difficult to use and understand.

Some professional words can not be replaced due to the exact meaning. For example, summon, subpoena, complaint, and indictment. These words can be used in writing to distinguish between other synonymous or close terms.

Some professional words are jargons which have the strict monosemy and used only in the special field of law. For example: imputed negligence, on the bench, take silk. On the one hand, the writer should avoid the meaning of these over-professional terms and use them carefully in writing, so as to avoid being too professional to cause difficulties for readers to understand.

4. Select simple words

Select simpler words and make sentences short. Read the following examples:

(1) Prior to 9/11, airport security was incomplete.

(2) Before 9/11, airport security was lax.

The second sentence is better. "Before" is a simpler word than "prior to", which is concise and easy to understand.

Other simple words are as follows:

adequate number of—sufficient

adjacent—next to

contained in—in

have an adverse impact on—harm

during the course of—during

To be simple and concise, redundant synonyms can be replaced by a simple word. There is no need to repeat the similar meaning.

For example:

null and void—void

fair and reasonable—fair

legal, valid, and binding—valid

true and correct—true

goods and chattels—chattels

fit and proper—proper

Meanwhile, the words need to be professional but need not to be over-professional. Some legal terms are Latin words or over-professional. They are not common in the current usage of English nowadays and they are difficult for readers to understand.

Read the following examples:

(1) This case is about lex loci.

(2) This case is about choice of law.

The second sentence is much easier for readers to understand.

Other over-professional words in writing can be replaced by simple words:

ad infinitum—indefinitely

id est—that is

inter alia—among others

per annum—per year

viva voca—orally

pro rata—proportionately

aforesaid—previous

forthwith—immediately

henceforth—now

herein—in this document

hereinafter—after this

thenceforth—after

thereafter—accordingly

hitherto—before

viz.—for example

whence—source

whereby—through

said—the/that

whilst—during

B. Voice

Voice is the tone of your document. In professional writing, the document's tone is formal. Selecting language that is not colloquial and avoiding slang are ways to ensure that the tone of the document is correct for the law firm or corporate legal department environment. The active voice emphasizes the actor. Active voice is the preferred voice because it is clearer, more concise and more lively than the passive voice.

Although the passive voice has its uses, it is generally wordier and not as strong as the active voice.

Read the following examples:

The initial quote for heat stamping equipment was rejected by Abbey.

Abbey rejected their initial quote for heat stamping equipment.

The second example is clear and more concise.

The passive voice, however, is sometimes acceptable. In some case cases, the person or thing performing the action is unknown.

For example:

Taxes were not deducted from his paychecks.

In other cases, the actor does not need to be mentioned because he or she is less important than the action. Compare the following examples:

(1) The action stems from a contract dispute in which goods were rejected by the defendant.

(2) The defendant rejected the goods, resulting in a contract dispute.

C. Paragraphs and Sentences

A paragraph is a collection of statements that focus on the same general subject. Effective paragraphs have a unified purpose, a thesis or topic sentence, and transitions between sentences. The topic sentences is generally the first sentence of a paragraph; it tells the readers the subject of the paragraph.

A sentence is a statement that conveys a single idea. It generally should be written in the active voice and must include a subject and a predicate.

1. The use of sentences in legal writing

a. Use more active sentences

The active sentence is more direct and convincing than the passive sentence. The passive sentences on express way are not so concise as the active sentences. Compare the following examples:

The court decided that the defendant's evidence was not enough.

It was decided that the defendant's evidence was not enough.

For the second sentence, it is not clear enough to determine who makes the decision.

In general, using passive sentences in the following situation is more appropriate: (1) to weaken the adverse legal fact. For example, in a criminal case, the defendant can state the fact by this way: *The claimant was hit by defendant.* On the contrary, the prosecution may use the active sentence: *The defendant hit the claimant.* Subject in the first part of a sentence is easy to cause readers' attention; (2) when it is not necessary to mention the actor; (3) when the subject is too long, to use the passive sentence can balance the structure; (4) when the object needs to be stressed.

b. Use more short sentences

Legal English needs to be concise and accurate. The writing needs to be smooth and clear. Therefore, it is important to avoid using complex long sentence structure which is difficult for readers to understand.

c. Use conjunctions to express logical relationship in long sentences

Although we emphasize on simplicity in legal writing, many places still need to use long sentences. Complicated long sentences can express the logical relationship by using appropriate conjunctions. For example:

The directors may, in their absolute discretion and without assigning any reason therefore, decline to register the transfer of a share, whether or not it is a fully paid share.

The use of "whether" directly expressed the logical relationship in this long sentence and made it easier to understand.

d. Use logic transition between sentences

Sentences should be connected to each other, and the internal logic between them should be shown to the readers as much as possible. Otherwise, it would be difficult for the readers to understand the writing. Therefore, the accurate logical transition of the structure becomes the key to describe the outline of logical relationship between each sentence.

Compare the following examples:

The litigation fees and counsel fees will cost more than the amount the claimant could receive if he wins the suit, although he has chosen to appeal.

The litigation fees and counsel fees will cost more than the amount the claimant could receive if he wins the suit. Nevertheless, he has chosen to appeal.

The second sentence is more logical and accurate by using the word of "nevertheless", which accurately shows the true meaning of the expression.

2. The common mistakes in writing sentences

a. Sentence fragment/Incomplete sentence

The essential elements of the sentence are omitted, such as subject or predicate. Compare the following examples:

The extent of the employer's control and supervision over the worker.

The court will consider the extent of the employer's control and supervision over the worker.

b. Run-on sentence

Another common mistake in drafting a sentence is when two sentences are combined without punctuation or by using a comma only.

(1) Compare the following examples:

The attorneys waited outside, the court was about to make its decision.

The attorneys waited outside. The court was about to make its decision.

(2) Compare the following examples:

There were ten findings of fact in the opinion, they all favored the plaintiff.

There were ten findings of fact in the opinion. All favored the plaintiff.

c. Unnecessary words

Review the following paragraph. Note that unnecessary words located.

The plaintiff (make a statement) that in his (own) opinion, during (the course of) (a period of) a year, the defendant (completely) destroyed the furniture the plaintiff hired the defendant to restore. The defendant failed to warn the plaintiff (in advance) that he couldn't restore the piece (properly) and that the price of the work originally estimated (roughly) at $500 would now cost her $1,500.

None of the words in parentheses add nothing to the reader's understanding of the sentences or paragraph.

Exercise:

Please explain accuracy with examples in legal writing.

Section 3   Punctuation

From the point of view of the readers, many readers with the impression of document form to determine whether the legal documents are professional, including punctuation.

The punctuation of a sentence, especially the placement of a comma, can change the meaning of that sentence. Therefore, you must carefully place each punctuation mark. The following provides you with some basic rules for checking your punctuation placement.

A. Commas

Commas tell a reader to pause. They are also used to set apart parenthetical phrases. In such a situation, commas should be used in pairs.

Read the following examples:

Molly ran to the school, the store, the basketball field, and then home. The defendant, George K., filed an answer to the complaint.

Now compare the following examples, and suppose your client has two sons, William and Ronald. She wants William to be the executor of the estate.

How should the document read?

I name my son William as the executor of my estate.

I name my son, William, as the executor of my estate.

Special comma rules include:

1. Commas separate a year from the date.

The plaintiff and the defendant agreed to the settlement on November 15, 2017.

2. Commas also set off the date from a specific reference to a day of the week.

The judge decided the summary judgment motion on Monday, November 7, 2015.

3. Commas separate a proper name from a title that follows it.

The plaintiff sued ATL Enterprises and Samuel Harris, company president.

4. Commas and periods should always appear inside quotation marks.

"But I wasn't in Tod on the night of the murder," the defendant protested.

"I was in Scotts with my elderly mother."

B. Semicolons

1. Semicolons are used to separate two independent sentences.

The paralegal's responsibilities are broad; they include summarization of depositions.

2. Semicolons separate clauses of a compound sentence when an adverbial conjunction joins the two.

The defendants presented a good case; however, they lost.

3. Semicolons are used to separate phrases in a list.

The committee members were Robert Harris, vice president of Harris Enterprises; Ana Williams, owner of Walworth Products; Barbara Halley, an attorney; and Benjamin Marcus, an accountant.

C. Colons

Colons are marks of introduction. Colons should appear only at the end of a main clause. They should never directly follow a verb or a preposition. Instead of saying *Marc loved many sports, such as: soccer, tennis, and baseball.*

The correct expression is *Marc loved many sports, such as soccer, tennis, and baseball.*

D. Parentheses

Parentheses tell the reader that the idea is an afterthought or is outside the main idea of a sentence.

The tort involved a banana peel (the classic culprit) and a crowded grocery store.

E. Double and Single Quotation Marks

Double quotation marks enclose direct quotations. Single quotation marks are used to define a quotation within a quotation.

The witness testified, "The robber said, 'Give me all your money.'"

F. Apostrophes

1. An apostrophe replaces letters that are omitted in contractions.

He's the defendant.

2. An apostrophe is also used with an 's to indicate the possessive case.

The defendant's car struck the plaintiff.

3. When a noun ends in an 's, the possessive case is indicated with only an apostrophe.

The attorney's clerks researched the applicable law.

4. To indicate a possessive for one item that two people share. However, use an apostrophe after each name if the item is not shared. Compare the following examples:

Ben and Sarah's motion is sound.

Ben's and Sarah's motion are sound.

5. Apostrophes are used to indicate plurals for numbers or letters.

The attorney told the defendant to watch his p's and q's in the courtroom.

Exercises:

1. Please edit the following sentences and name the grammar mistakes.

(1) The jury were to eat lunch at noon.

(2) The attorney and the paralegal was available for the client.

(3) The paralegal association set the following goals: recruitment of new members, educating the community, and improvement of paralegal work conditions. (were-collective nouns; were-compound subjects; education—follow the same grammatical pattern or number)

2. Please find out the professional words that can be used in writing from the text and try to explain these words.

The attorney explained that some factors should be considered before deciding on the forum. Bob might bring the suit in several places: (a)in a state trial court where Bob lives; (b)in a state trial court where Eric lives; (c)in a state trial court where the estate is located; (d)in the federal trial court sitting in Bob's state; (e)in the federal trial court sitting in the Eric's state, or; (f) in the federal trial court sitting in the state where the estate is located. The reason Bob could sue in a federal court was the existence of diversity of citizenship. The suit would be brought in the U.S. District Court sitting in Bob's own state since this would be most convenient venue for Bob.

Answer:

(1) Form: A court which has jurisdiction to hold a trial of a particular lawsuit or petition.

(2) Estate: All the property left by a decedent from which any obligations or debts of the decedent must be paid.

(3) Diversity of citizenship: A kind of jurisdiction giving a federal court the power to

hear a case based upon the fact that (a) the parties to the litigation are from different states, and; (b)the amount of money involved exceeds the amount usually $7,500.

(4) Venue: The proper or most convenient location for trial of a case. Normally, the venue in a criminal case is the judicial district or county where the crime was committed. For civil cases, venue is usually the district which is the residence of a principal defendant, where a contract was executed or is to performed, or where an accident took place.

Chapter 12
Legal Writing in General

法律文书是法律专业人员提供服务工作的主要载体。一般来说，法律咨询或其他法律服务最终会以书面形式体现出来，如咨询函、合同、信函、诉讼文书等。在学习了前一章通用写作的基础上，本章更侧重于法律写作的思维与步骤，是对常见的法律文书类型写作共同要求的概括和介绍。

本章介绍了法律写作的一般步骤，详细介绍了描述和适用法律时的要点，强调了法律写作中分析的主要方面，并介绍了采用段落和主题句等方法使法律行文更有逻辑且重点突出。本章还具体介绍了法律写作中进行探讨和论述的思路和要点以及法律写作中常用的 IRAC 方法等内容。

Different legal documents are produced in the process of legal professional for service of the main carrier of the work. Normally, legal advice or other legal services will ultimately reflect in the written form, such as the consultation letter, contract, letter, and lawsuit documents, which requires a clear and rigorous thinking. On the basis of general writing skills in the previous chapter, this chapter focuses more on the thinking and steps of legal writing. In legal writing, the application of the previous chapter is also indispensable.

Section 1 Organization

A good piece of legal writing does not require the reader to figure things out for himself or herself. Apart from careful planning, there are six basic principles of good organization that will enable you to create a document that is easy to read and easy to understand. Meanwhile, drafting legal documents does not amount to merely changing the names, dates, or other specific information of parties in a standard or precedent text. We need to solve the problem of specific analysis according to the requirements of the parties. Standard texts or previous examples can be used as a reference to help you quickly grasp the common points of similar problems.

A. Address "Givens" at the Outset of Analysis

Any legal analysis requires a thorough explanation of how the law applies to the facts. Meanwhile, the facts need to be correctly stated. You may get much information about the fact from your client or by your own research. However, you need to determine whether the facts are logical and useful. If not sure, you need to ask the relevant parties for further inquiries to clarify the facts. The more complex the fact, the more attention must be paid to presentation and analysis. If the basis of the analysis is wrong, then subsequent analyses of legal writing are likely to be wrong.

Keep in mind, however, that not all elements of a particular rule require the same level of analysis. When you need to analyze a rule that involves multiple elements, you will often find that some of them are "givens".

B. Discuss Each Issue Separately

Before discussing each issue, the beginning of the legal document can introduce the overall idea of the writing, so that the reader can understand the whole topic and order of the paper. Especially, in the case of many issues need to analyze. The introduction of the overall idea at the beginning not only enables the reader to intuitively understand the main points of the document, but also helps him or her not to deviate from the idea of the text.

When there are two or more issues that merit analysis, you must examine each separately. Discuss and draw a conclusion about one issue before moving to the next. Distinct separation of issues helps the reader understand the issues and sharpen his or her understandings as well.

C. Discuss Each Sub-issue Separately

Each issue, as you have discovered, often has several parts or sub-issues. Each sub-issue involves its own rule, and thus its own set of significant facts. You should deal with each sub-issue in sequence, finishing the discussion of one before continuing to the next.

It is necessary to use unified and distinct serial number identification to mark the issues, which can clearly and intuitively show the analysis and conclusion of each issue.

D. Describe the Applicable Law Before Applying It to the Factual Situation

Each issue or sub-issue involves the application of a legal rule to specific facts. The relevant legal rules, therefore, provide a framework for your analysis and should be stated first. If you state the facts concerning an issue or sub-issue first, without describing the applicable law, the facts will mean nothing to your reader.

E. State the Reasons Supporting Your Conclusion Before Discussing Counterarguments

The result of your thinking on an issue or sub-issue should be a legal conclusion. This conclusion should be expressed in your thesis. After stating your thesis, explain the reasons for it. You may have come to understand reasons only after thoughtful analysis.

In addition, the meaning of relevant words should be consistent throughout the writing process. It is a good way to define specific terms as they first appear and remain uniform throughout the text. The reader will be able to understand the connection between different matters when reading the document without confusing relevant concepts or affecting the understanding of the analysis.

F. Analyze the Risks of the Solution

When your response to a client involves a solution to a problem, it is better to analyze the risks involved in the solution and inform the client of the basis for your judgment. Legal professions face many problems which are not black-and-white answers. There are many problems in the gray area with uncertainty. Therefore, if the parties still insisted the implementation of a solution, you shall inform the relevant risks. For the parties concerned, each legal risks faced could be converted into the corresponding business risks and even serious risks. Therefore, the consulting documents issued to a party should have a full discussion about risks and reasons. Finally, the client can choose to bear which risk degree according to himself.

G. Organize the Issue Logically

During the writing process, you need to connect and organize each part in a logical way so that the reader can understand that you have properly considered all relevant factors. In addition, it is necessary to follow up and avoid unnecessary content repetition and meaningless tautology. If the resolution of one issue depends on the resolution of another issue, the initial or threshold issue belongs first. Your reader will understand your analysis better if you write that way. Your reader will also not wonder whether you assumed away a large question without even analyzing it.

Exercises:

1. *Please share thoughts on separating issues in legal writing.*
2. *Please restate steps for good organization in legal writing.*

Section 2 Describe the Law

Drafting legal documents is not equivalent to list or copy the provisions of laws and rules. It is not legal writing, but simply copying. The description of the law must convey to your reader the essential legal rules or principles your discussion is based on, and it must fit well with the rest of the discussion. A good explanation of the law makes your analysis credible to your reader.

A. Be Accurate

An accurate explanation will enable the reader to understand precisely what the law says, and will provide a logical and coherent basis for the analysis that follows. Readers will often want to study the relevant cases, statutes, or constitutional provisions for themselves. Accuracy is also important in legal writing because of the precise meaning given to many words and phrases. The difference between similar sounding words and phrases can be substantial.

B. Describe Only the Relevant Law

Describe only the law that may affect the outcome of the client's case. If common law is relevant, describe only the rules, facts, holdings and reasons and policies that are relevant to the issue or sub-issue being analyzed. If a statue is relevant, describe only that portion of the statute that may apply to your client's situation.

C. Describe the Law in Enough Detail

You should be able to analyze each issue or sub-issue solely on the basis of your written explanation of the law, without going to the law itself. Likewise, your reader should be able to independently analyze the issue solely from your description of the law.

D. Summarize the Law Whenever Appropriate

In any discussion of a legal issue, you must identify the sources of the legal rules you apply. How much information you must give about the source of a rule varies. If you are setting out a general and undisputed legal principle, such as in an introductory statement to move the reader from the broad area of the law to the narrow issue under consideration, a bare citation to a case or statute is usually sufficient.

E. Synthesize the Law Whenever Necessary

It is sometimes necessary to synthesize several authorities in order to create a complete description of law. You will often find that several highly relevant cases support your position or that several cases need to be distinguished.

Exercise:

Please explain basic principles for describing the law.

Section 3　Explaining the Analysis

After you describe the law supporting your position, you will explain how the law actually supports your position. The discussion and analysis of the issue is the core content of the whole writing. Similarly, after you describe the law that might support a counterargument, you will explain how the law fails to support that counterargument. The writer needs to combine law and the facts for each issue to conduct a comprehensive and detailed analysis. For continental law countries, the writing must be accurate reference statute law and relevant judicial interpretations. If necessary, it also needs to refer to authoritative scholars' point of view or national policy. For Common Law countries, in addition to the practice of continental law countries above, it also needs a large number of reference cases. When citing cases, you need to be careful to compare the similar cases, which are called "the ability to distinguish cases".

A. Be Precise

Effective communication is directly related to the care with which words are chosen and sentences and paragraphs are structured.

B. Show Every Step in the Analysis

Because memos are written for lawyers, it is safe to assume that the reader will have a basic understanding of the law and the legal process.

C. Describe Every Reasonable Basis for Your Conclusion

Take care to include only the most persuasive or effective reasons or theories. A good test is whether each reason or theory could stand on its own without support from the others. If so, it is probably worth including.

D. Explain the Context

When the importance of a legal issue or sub-issue to the resolution of a problem may not be apparent to the reader, you must explain how that issue or sub-issue fits into the factual situation and how it relates to the rights and responsibilities of those involved.

Exercise:

Explain the importance of explaining the context in legal writing.

Section 4 Signposting

Signposting is especially important in legal writing because of the nature of your audience and the circumstances under which your document will be read. There are four types of signposts: thesis statements, paragraphs, topic sentences and transitions.

A. Use Thesis Statements

A thesis is a sentence in the first or second paragraph of a formal paper that states the writer's conclusion. It gives the reader a foundation for reading and understanding the paper. A clear opening thesis tells the reader what to look for and what to focus on.

B. Use Paragraphs

A paragraph is a group of sentences relating to one discrete idea or topic. The proper use of paragraphs helps to divide the discussion into parts that can be readily understood. Proper paragraphing is especially important in legal documents because of their complexity and the circumstance in which they are read.

C. Use a Topic Sentence

Just as a thesis sentence summarizes your basic point or conclusion on a issue or sub-issue, a topic sentence explains the basic points of a paragraph and thus provides a frame of reference for what is to follow. It is usually the first or second sentence of a paragraph.

D. Use Transitions

Transactions are the directions the writer uses to guide the reader from one part of the discussion to another. Transitions signal to the reader that you have completed the discussion of one point and are proceeding to the next. Here are some examples of transitional words and phrases for each of these:

Relationship Between Ideas	Transitional Words & Phrases
Similarity between the previous point and the next one	similarity, also, in addition further/furthermore moreover
Difference between the previous point and the next one	however, nevertheless/nonetheless although, on the other hand, in contrast
Enumeration of points	first, second, third, etc. finally, last
Causal relationship	consequently, therefore, thus, because
Temporal relationship	subsequently, previously later, in the meantime, then, recently

Exercise:

Explain the function of signposting via the sentence "Tell your reader where you are going, and then clearly and carefully guide the reader as you go."

Section 5 Drafting the Discussion

Legal writing differs from the kind of writing you probably did as an undergraduate. The three main differences are: its purpose, the process and the audience.

The following charts below illustrates both the linear approach and the recursive approach.

Liner Approach
Identify and narrow issues
Research
Analyze and organize
Write
Rewrite

Recursive Approach
Identify the issues—Plan your research—Begin your research
Analyze research—Narrow issues—Organize
Research—Analyze research—Write
Analyze again—Rewrite
Research—Rewrite
Rewrite

As you gain experience in legal writing, you will learn to recognize situations in which some deviation from the structure suggested here may result in a more cogent discussion.

A. State the Conclusion First

State your conclusion on any specific issue at the outset. Stating your conclusion first serves two purposes. First, it ensures that you have actually reached a conclusion. It is difficult, if not impossible, to begin writing a discussion of a legal issue until you have sorted out how the law applies to the relevant facts.

B. State the Conclusion Based on Rules

This step requires you to state your conclusion for each sub-issue that arises under an issue. Like the first one, this step ensures that you have actually reached a conclusion and makes it easier for the reader to follow your discussion. Again, your conclusion should include both the relevant legal rule and the significant facts.

C. Describe the Law Relevant to the Conclusion

For common law problems, state the general rule first and then describe cases relevant to your conclusion that apply the rule. For statutory problems, quote or summarize the relevant provision first and then explain how any judicial decisions may have modified, extended, restricted or defined the statute.

D. Explain the Supporting Reasons

Once you have stated your conclusion and the relevant law, you must explain the reasons for your conclusion. This explanation is the most important part of your discussion and should include evert step in your reasoning process as well as every reasonable basis for your conclusion.

E. Describe Reasonable Counterargument

When you state your reasons for rejecting an opposite conclusion, you begin your response to potential counterarguments and signal to the reader that you are moving to a different part of the discussion.

F. Describe the Law Supports the Counterargument

To be even minimally credible, opposing arguments require some legal basis. The description of the law that supports your conclusion should be complete enough for the reader to understand the relevant cases or statutory provisions, but you must also explain how the law supports the counterargument.

G. Explain Reason for the Unchanged Conclusion

Once you have set out the law on which the counterargument would be based, you must explain why the counterargument is less convincing than your conclusion. Be sure to address the strongest counterarguments. A writer gains credibility by acknowledging and refuting the most difficult 146 counterarguments, not by constructing and refuting weak or insupportable arguments.

H. Edit the Discussion to Include Signposts

The first seven steps provide a structure for developing your discussion. The first, second and fifth steps—in which you state your conclusion on the issue, your conclusion on the sub-issue, and your response to a potential counterargument—tell your reader where you are going. But these steps, by themselves, do not necessarily ensure that your reader understand the discussion supporting your conclusion or your discussion of the counterargument.

Exercises:

1. Please compare linear approach and recursive approach in your own words.
2. Please explain basic steps for discussion structure.

Section 6 IRAC Method

Analyzing cases or citing cases to support your conclusions are very common and important in legal writing. IRAC method is often used in case analysis. "I" stands for "Issue". "R" stands for "Rule". "A" stands for "Application" or "Analysis". "C" stands for "Conclusion". When using the IRAC method, do not forget the writing points highlighted in the previous section.

A. Introduction to IRAC

1. Issue

The IRAC starts with a statement of the issues or legal questions at hand. In the issue section of an IRAC, it is important to state exactly what the question of law is. Again, each issue is often discussed separately mentioned before. The "Whether ... when" or "Under (law) ... does" formats may be of service in framing the issue.

The statement of issues in writing is also known as "the questions presented". Issues can be divided into two aspects: One is called the issue of facts and another is called the issue of law. The former refers to the fact that exists or not and how to take place in the disputes. The latter refers to the legal provisions and the controversy of application.

The statement of issue is usually written in short inductive language. When setting a focus, be sure to consider the full range of possibilities in your writing.

2. Rule

The Rule section of an IRAC follows the statement of the issue at hand. The rule section of an IRAC is the statement of the rules pertinent in deciding the issue stated. Rules in a common law jurisdiction derive from court case precedent and statute. The information included in the rules section depends heavily on the specificity of the question at hand. If the question states a specific jurisdiction, then it is proper to include rules specific to that jurisdiction. Another distinction often made in the rule section is a clear delineation of rules that are in holding, and binding based on the authority of the hierarchy of the court, being ratio decidendi, and being the majority ruling, or simply persuasive. There are occasions when rules are adopted on the basis that they are the only clearly articulated rules on the issue, in spite of being minority decisions, obiter dicta, and from lower courts, in other jurisdictions, which have never been contradicted.

The rules help make a correct legal analysis of the issue at hand using the facts of the case. The rules section needs to be a legal summary of all the rules used in the analysis and is often written in a manner which paraphrases or otherwise analytically condenses information into applicable rules.

3. Application

The Application (or Analysis) section of an IRAC applies the rules developed in the rules section to the specific facts of the issue at hand. This section uses only the rules stated in the rules section of the IRAC and usually utilizes all the rules stated including exceptions as is required by the analysis. It is important in this section to apply the rules to the facts of the case and explain or argue why a particular rule applies or does not apply in the case presented. The application/analysis section is the most important section of an IRAC because it develops the answer to the issue at hand. It is useful to think like a lawyer, and argue the facts from both sides using the rules before offering a decision or coming to a conclusion.

4. Conclusion

The Conclusion section of an IRAC directly answers the question presented in the issue section of the IRAC. It is important for the methodology of the IRAC that the conclusion section of the IRAC not introduce any new rules or analysis. This section restates the issue and provides the final answer.

Conclusion is not a short answer to each issue or simple repetition. The main difference is that a conclusion focuses on the whole case and makes overall prediction, including the person's strengths and weaknesses as well as the possibility to win. The short answer is just a brief answer to each issue.

B. Variations

There exist some proponents and opponents against IRAC. The main arguments of the proponents of the IRAC methodology say it reduces legal reasoning to the application of a formula that helps organize the legal analysis. In order to avoid the strict and unwieldy format

of IRAC. The alternative versions of the IRAC have appeared. For example:
- FIRAC (Facts, Issues, Relevant Legal Provisions and Rules, Application of Rules, Conclusion).
- MIRAT (Material Facts, Issues, Rules, Application, Tentative Conclusion).
- IDAR (Issues, Doctrine, Application, Result).
- CRAAC [Conclusion, Rules, Analogous Case (if applicable), Application, Conclusion]. This is mostly used for writing assignments.
- CREAC (Conclusion, Rules, Explanation, Application, Conclusion)
- TREACC (Topic, Rule, Explanation, Analysis, Counterarguments, Conclusion)
- TRIAccC [Topic, Rule, Issues, Analysis (cases, conclusion), Conclusion]
- TREAT [Thesis, Rule, (Rule) Explanation, (Rule) Application, Thesis]
- TRRAC (Thesis, Rule Statement, Rule Explanation, Application, Conclusion)
- CRuPAC (Conclusion, Rule, Proof, Analysis, Conclusion)
- ILAC (Issue, Law, Application, Conclusion)
- CIRAC (Conclusion, Issue, Rules, Application, Conclusion)
- IPAAC (Issue, Principle, Authority, Application, Conclusion)
- IRREAC (Issue, Rule, Rule Explanation, Application, Conclusion)
- CLEO (Claim, Law, Evaluation, Outcome)
- IRACDD (Issue, Rule, Analysis, Conclusion, Defense, Damages)

Although there are different names and structures, these methods are generally combined with objective statements of fact, in accordance with the law to analyze the issue and to get the final conclusion. The ideas and main points of this process are highlighted in this chapter.

C. Example of IRAC

Read the following cases and the analysis by the IRAC method.

Mike walks into a store and picks up a book. He then stuffs the book beneath his jacket. A security attendant sees him and follows him to the cash register. Mike passes through without stopping to pay for anything. The security attendant stops him at the gate. He detains Mike while he interrogates him. Mike is unresponsive and uncooperative and in fact downright hostile to the charges being leveled at him by the security attendant. Mike is held for a period of two hours at the end of which it is found that he had actually put the book back and was not stealing. Mike sues the grocery store for false imprisonment. Would Mike prevail in court?

1. Issue

The issue here is whether Mike could prevail in court by alleging that he was falsely imprisoned.

2. Rules

Most jurisdictions in the United States allow recovery for false imprisonment. The courts look at two elements in determining whether a person has been falsely imprisoned: just cause and authority.

(1) For the element of just cause, courts further analyze two factors: reasonable suspicion and the environment in which the actions take place.

① If a person suspects that he is being deprived of property legally attached to him and he can show that his suspicions are reasonable, then he is said to have a reasonable suspicion.

② Courts also look at whether the activity in question took place in an environment where stealing is common. Crowded public places and shops are considered to be more justifiable places where a person could have just cause for reasonable suspicion in comparison to private property or sparsely populated areas.

(2) For the element of authority

① The courts tend to favor people directly charged with handling security as people with the authority to detain a person in comparison to private individuals.

② The courts have made exceptions in the favor of the person conducting the detention if he is a shopkeeper. This special privilege is called the shopkeeper's privilege.

③ In general the element of authority is usually seen as one part of a two part legal justification for legally justifiable detention. For example, in cases involving detention by an officer of the law, courts have ruled that the officer has to have both just cause and authority.

④ Authority in itself is not enough. The same reasoning applies to all detaining individuals. Exceptions are made in the case where a person of authority has to conduct an investigation with just cause and courts usually grant a reasonable amount of time in detention for this purpose. Here the reasonable amount of time a person can be kept in detention is directly related to the circumstances under which the detention takes place.

3. Application/Analysis

Mike was conducting his activity in a crowded place that happened to be a grocery store. He was further detained by a security attendant. The security attendant had seen him pick up a loaf of bread and walk past the cash register without paying. The security attendant detained him until he discovered that no theft had taken place. Mike was subsequently released upon this determination of fact.

(1) The first element of false imprisonment is just cause.

① The first factor of just cause is reasonable suspicion.

The security attendant saw Mike pick up the book and stuff it beneath his jacket. This is an uncommon action as most shop customers usually do not hide produce under their personal belongings. The security attendant has reasonable suspicion because a reasonable person in his place would have also considered this action to be suspicious. Mike further walks by the cash register without paying. A reasonable person in the security attendant's stead would arguably act to stop Mike. Thus, this seems to satisfy the first factor of the element of just cause, reasonable suspicion.

② The second factor of the element of just cause is the environment

A store is usually a place where shoplifters and other thieves operate regularly. This reduces the burden of just cause placed on the person performing the detention. The security attendant has to be unusually vigilant and suspicious of a person's motive because of his location. This then seems to satisfy the second factor of the element of just cause, environment.

(2) The second element of false imprisonment is authority.

The security attendant is the person charged with securing the grocery store and its property. The security attendant performs the investigation after he puts Mike in detention and it takes two hours. Two hours might seem like an unreasonable amount of time but given the fact that Mike was unresponsive and uncooperative it seems to be reasonable. It also seems as if the security attendant was doing his due diligence as he releases person Mike as soon as the facts are established and it is shown that Mike was not stealing the loaf of bread.

(3) The shopkeeper's privilege applies directly to the security attendant

This privilege gives the security attendant extra leeway in detaining people in whom he has reasonable suspicion. Most courts would lean heavily towards the shopkeeper because Mike was on the property of the store and thus could be subjected to extra scrutiny given the long history of the shopkeeper's privilege in common law.

4. Conclusion

Mike would most likely not prevail in the courts because the security attendant does not satisfy either element of false imprisonment. The detention of Mike was legal because the security attendant had both just cause and authority. Additionally, the shopkeeper's privilege further solidifies the legality of the detention.

Exercise:

Please explain and make comments on IRAC Method.

Section 7   Revising and Editing

Almost everything you need to know about writing can be summarized in one principle: Write to communicate. Revising and editing are essential to both the substance and the style of your writing. In fact, in the process of correction and proofreading, many points are already mentioned in the previous chapter. These points are best addressed at the time of writing to reduce the burden of later revisions. This section again highlights some very important caveats.

A. Be Direct and Precise

To make sure that your writing is as direct and precise as possible, review your draft paragraph by paragraph, word by word. In writing and editing, you should find that your thinking and consequently your memo or brief becomes increasingly clear and focused.

B. Blend Precision with Simplicity

As you strive for precision, be careful to state your ideas as simply as possible. Avoid jargon, legalese and Latin phrases as well as long words, sentences and paragraphs. Persons untrained in the law should be able to read and understand your writing.

C. Be Concise

Avoid wordy phrases, avoid tautological phrases and avoid unnecessary modifiers. Scrutinize sentences beginning with "there" or "it".

Eliminate unnecessary information and repetition. Avoid redundancies, avoid extraneous facts. For example, the following words and sentences are useless:

obviously, clearly, manifestly ...

It is obvious that ...

It is clear that ...

As a matter of fact

To tell the truth

Situation is where ...

Case is when ...

D. Edit Intrusive or Misplaced Words and Phrases

Modifying words and phrases should generally be as close as possible to the words or phrases they modify. The more words that come between these elements, the greater the risk that the sentence will not say what you intend.

E. Use Correct Grammar, Punctuation and Spelling

Minor errors distract the reader from the message to be conveyed. Major errors may distort the message or make it unintelligible. In either case, the communication between the writer and the reader is interrupted. Always proofread your sentences to make sure they are technically correct, even if you begin by using spell-checking programs on your word processor.

Exercise:

Please compare which statement is more clear and forceful.

(1) The department shall disclose all relevant information to the requesting party.

(2) All relevant information shall be disclosed to the requesting party.

Chapter 13
Correspondence

在法律实务中，高效、优质的信函写作技巧有助于提升法律事务的处理和日常商务沟通效率。信函写作要求写作者对语气、组织等有清晰的认知。信函中细节因素的相互作用往往对信函整体效果的呈现有较大的影响。即使是在数字经济高速发展的今天，包括电子邮件等方式在内的信函沟通依然是商业交往的远程沟通主流方式。充分了解信函的沟通内容与技巧将有助于推动法律服务行业的规范化与专业化。本章内容包括信函的基本架构、信函类型、信函写作用语等方面，提炼了法律信函写作中需要关注的重点，并为读者提供了相关的写作技巧。

Great letter writing is an art. The right touch with tone, organization and level of formality requires a clear eye and ear. Although the individual factors in a piece of correspondence are easily understood, the interaction of those factors is so complex that the exact effect defies easy prediction. Although good letter writing can be learned, great letter writing cannot be reduced to a dry set of rules.

Section 1 Components of a Letter

A letter is divided into several sections: the date, the name and the address of the addressee called the inside address, a reference line, a greeting to the addressee, the body of the letter and the complimentary closing.

A. Letterhead and Headers

Draft the first page of a letter on firm letterhead. The letterhead is the portion of the firm's stationery that identifies the firm. It usually includes the firm's address, its telephone and facsimile numbers. Additional pages should not carry the firm letterhead but should be placed on matching paper with a header on each page.

B. Date

The date should be placed at the top of the letter just below the firm's letterhead. The date is one of the key components of a letter concerning any legal matters. Date the letter with the same date as the date of mailing. This date can be crucial in determining a time line in a legal proceeding.

C. Inside Address

The next part of the letter, the inside address, should contain the name of the person to whom the letter is addressed, the individual's title if he or she has one, the name of the business if the letter is for a business and the address.

D. Reference Line

The reference line is a brief statement regarding the topic of the letter. Some firms ask the reference line contain a client number, claim number or case number, so investigate your firm's style.

For example,

Re: Sale of commercial property—214 Barrington Road, Toledo, Ochio

E. Greeting

In general, your greeting depends on how familiar you are with an individual. If you know an individual well, you may address, formally, such that person by the first name. If you are uncertain whether to address the individual by the first name, use a title and the individual's last name. If you are addressing a letter to a person, but you do not know the person's name, try to determine the person's name.

F. Body of the Letter

The body of the letter follows the greeting and should begin with an opening sentence and paragraph that summarizes the purpose of the letter.

Draft the body of the letter carefully. Outline the letter before writing it to be sure that you address all necessary points.

Regardless of its length or complexity, a good body of letter always needs three basic parts:

1. An opening, which orients the reader to the letter's purpose and the writer's tone;
2. A middle, which delivers the content with needed support or explanation; and
3. An ending, which closes politely while reaffirming the writer's original tone and purpose.

This three-part structure breaks letter writing into three manageable pieces that can be adapted for all sorts of correspondence structures, as Table 13-1 illustrates.

Table 13-1 How the Three-Part Structure Applies to Various Types of Letters

Contents of Letter	Orient the Reader	Deliver the Message	Close Consistently
Giving good news	State the news.	Elaborate as needed.	Close politely.
Answering a request	Refer to request.	Answer and Explain.	Say whom to contact with questions.
Making a routine request	Identify self and make request.	List what is needed.	Thank the reader.
Making a special request	Explain why you are making the request.	Make request, with list as needed.	Thank the reader and explain how to reach you if there are questions.
Giving Directions	Overview task.	Explain tasks step by step.	Explain what to do if the reader has problems.
Persuading to take action	Refer to the background that puts the writer in a position to recommend.	State the recommendation and reasons.	Refer to recommendation and action it would require.
Cover letter	Refer to project to which materials relate.	List what is enclosed.	Refer to project at which materials will be used.
Answering a complaint	Summarize the complaint.	Answer and explain.	Explain the next step if appropriately and politely close.
Giving bad news	Establish your role with the reader.	State the news and explain.	Echo the role established in the first paragraph.

G. Closing

End your letter with a closing in which you invite a response, such as

Please do not hesitate to call if you have any questions.

or thank the address for assistance, such as

Thank you in advance for your cooperation.

Finally, end the letter with a complimentary closing such as

Sincerely, Very truly yours, Best regards,

Place two lines below the final line of the body of the letter.

Place your name four lines below the closing to allow a signature.

H. Copies to Others and Enclosures

If you are copying a third party on the letter and want the original addressee to know this, note it with cc (carbon copy). If you do not want the original addressee to know that you copied a letter to another letter, note it with *bcc* (blind carbon copy). The next notation is for enclosures (Enc. or Encs.), such as contracts, court orders or releases.

Finally, the letter should note your initials in all capital letters as the author of the letter and then the initials in lowercase letters of the person who typed the letter.

There is a general sample:

Contact Information *(Include your contact information unless you are writing on letterhead that already includes it.)*

Your Name

Your Address

Your City, State Zip Code

Your Phone Number

Your Email Address

Date

Contact Information *(The person or company you are writing to)*

Exercise:

Please kindly mark the components of the following illustration letter.

Full Block Letter

Fuzzwell, Cubbon and Landefelt

888 Toledo Road

Ottawa Hills, Ohio 43606

(419)535-7738

November 7, 2012

Via Federal Express

Mr. Stuart Shulman

Navarre Industries

708 Anthony Wayne Trail

Maumee, Ohio 45860

Re: Settlement of Kramer v. Shulman

Dear Mr. Shulman,

I have enclosed a copy of the settlement agreement that we drafted and that has

> been signed by Mr. Kramer. Please sign the agreement and forward it to me at the above address by November 30, 2012.
>
> If you have any questions, please feel free to call me at 535-7738.
>
> Sincerely,
Mara Cubbon
Legal Assistant
>
> cc: Randall Fuzzwell
> Enc.
> MAC/wlk

Section 2　Communication Tone

To write effective correspondence, focus on both content and tone. Correspondence communicates not only the writer's message, but also how the writer views the reader. The following two e-mail messages communicate quite different relationships, although the content is similar.

Message 1:

I have attached two sample contract forms for your review, as we discussed over the phone. The first is the shorter one, while the second addresses more contingencies. These should help you become more familiar with the range of choices we will be discussing in our planning meeting next week. Please contact me if I can help further.

Message 2:

Attached please find two standard form contracts per our conversation via phone, one shorter and the other covering more contingencies, representative of the range of choices upcoming at our next meeting.

The first version communicates courtesy and friendliness, and the reader is left with a positive feeling about the writer. The second version sounds unappealing with its use of bureaucratic phrases like "attached please find" and "per our conversation". Overall, the second version creates the impression that the writer wants create distance from the reader.

Regarding formal or informal stance toward the reader, the choices are generally subtle on this dimension. For example, avoid both of the following because they are too extreme.

It would be appreciated if you would sign the enclosed copy and return it to me in the envelope enclosed herewith. Your assistance in this matter is appreciated.

Just sign it, stuff it, and send it back. See ya!

You might use either of the following.

Please sign and return the enclosed copy of this agreement in the enclosed envelope. I appreciate your assistance in this matter.

Just sign the copy and return it to me in the enclosed envelope. Thank you for your help.

Here are some examples in expressing different levels of formality, including too causal mode, appropriate mode and too formal mode.

Table 13-2 Different Levels of Formality

T-Shirt=too causal	Business Casual to Business Suit=appropriate	Tuxedo=too formal
about that case	regarding that case	as to that case
soused, snockered, feeling no pain, etc.	drunk intoxicated	inebriated
a whole bunch of, a lot of	many	myriad, a great number of
think about chew on	consider	give consideration to
clear up	explain clarify	elucidate
being that	because	in the situation where
given that	if	in the event that
can't	cannot	lacks the capacity to
didn't cut it didn't pass muster flunked bombed	failed did not succeed was ineffective was inefficacious	attempted in vain came to naught
might try take a shot at	could try	make an attempt to
say that	argue that	make the argument that
settle on	agree	concur

(To be continued)

T-Shirt=too causal	Business Casual to Business Suit=appropriate	Tuxedo=too formal
in a jam	have a problem	discomfited
over with	ended	concluded
give a hand	help assist	faciliate
p.o'ed	angry irritated	infuriated in a pique
gave in to	agreed to gave consent consented to	acquiesced to acceded to
shell out	pay, reimburse	remunerate

Compare the tone and formality of two letters.

Example 1:

Nicole Thomas

35 Chestnut Street, Dell Village, Wisconsin 54101

nicolethomas@gmail.com

May 6, 2020

Jason Andrews

Manager

LMK Company

53 Oak Avenue, Ste 5

Dell Village, Wisconsin 54101

Dear Jason,

 I'm writing to resign my position as customer service representative, effective June 15, 2020.

 I've recently decided to go back to school, and my program starts in early September. I'm tendering my resignation now so that I can be as helpful as possible to you during the transition.

> I've truly enjoyed my time working with you and everyone else on our team at LMK. It's rare to find a customer service role that offers as much opportunity to grow and learn and such a positive, inspiring team of people to grow and learn with.
>
> I'm particularly grateful for your guidance while I was considering furthering my education. Your support has meant so much to me.
>
> Please let me know if there's anything I can do to help you find and train my replacement.
>
> Thanks, and best wishes,
>
> Nicole Thomas

(In this example, Nicole knows Jason Andrews well enough to use his first name in the salutation.)

Example 2:

> Nicole Thomas
> 35 Chestnut Street
> Dell Village, Wisconsin 54101
> nicolethomas@gmail.com
>
> August 3, 2020
>
> Jason Andrews
> Manager
> LMK Company
> 53 Oak Avenue, Ste 5
> Dell Village, Wisconsin 54101
>
> Dear Jason,
>
> I'm writing to resign from my position as customer service representative, effective August 14, 2020.
>
> I've recently decided to go back to school, and my program starts in early September.

> I'm tendering my resignation now so that I can be as helpful as possible to you during the transition.
>
> I've truly enjoyed my time working with you and everyone else on our team at LMK. It's rare to find a customer service role that offers as much opportunity to grow and learn, as well as such a positive, inspiring team of people to grow and learn with.
>
> I'm particularly grateful for your guidance while I was considering furthering my education. Your support has meant so much to me.
>
> Please let me know if there's anything I can do to help you find and train my replacement.
>
> Thanks, and best wishes,
>
> Nicole Thomas (signature hard copy letter)
> Nicole Thomas

(To compare with the last one, this example is more professional and formal.)

Exercises:

Please modify the following inconsistent writing styles.

1. I know this whole situation really stinks.
2. If you find this alternative acceptable, please sign the enclosed release form and bring it back right away.
3. I know this situation has been discouraging for you.
4. If you find this alternative acceptable, please sign the enclosed release form and return it to our office so that we may proceed.

Section 3　Types of Letters

A. Confirming Letters

Confirming letters reaffirm information already agreed to by you and the recipient. It is a good practice to follow up any conversation with a client or an opposing attorney or paralegal with a confirming letter that summarizes the conversation, any agreements made, or any future acts to be accomplished.

For example, the following is a letter confirming the content of the meeting:

Dear Mr. Smith:

Thank you for taking the time to meet with us yesterday to discuss the progress on your case. At the outset, I must say I thought the meeting was very productive for all of us. Here, I would like to go over the major issues that we discussed and the decisions we made yesterday.

First, you have authorized us to engage the services of an outside counsel to assist in this matter. As we discussed yesterday, there will be no direct cost to you for these services. It is our intention to enter into a written agreement wherein the outside counsel will receive a portion of the attorneys' fees due to this firm in the event that we prevail on the case. Additionally, it is my intention to seek contribution from the outside counsel for ongoing expenses in an amount proportionate to our fee agreement with them.

You also authorized us to retain the services of a second expert witness. As you know, this expert has requested a RMB 8,000.00 retainer, and it is my intention to engage his services in the very near future.

We also discussed a budget for expenses in this case. At the present time, my prediction is that total expenses could very well be in the range of RMB 200,000.00 if we have to complete formal discovery and prepare for trial. You were kind enough to agree to pay 100% of all of the expenses thus incurred.

Finally, following a discussion of the pros and cons of mediation and arbitration, you have authorized us to attempt to arrange a non-binding mediation with the defendant. As we discussed, I anticipate that our share of the expenses for the mediation would be RMB 4,000.00. I will attempt to make the necessary arrangements as soon as possible.

I hope that this letter accurately reflects the decisions we made yesterday. If not, I would be most appreciative if you could let me know at your earliest convenience.

Sincerely,
Mara Cubbon

B. Status Letters and Transaction Summary Letters

Often you will be asked to provide a status report of a case, especially to insurance companies and other clients. These letters provide clients with an overview of the current activities in a court case, transaction, or other legal matters.

Transaction summary letters often follow a business transaction such as a real estate closing. In these letters, you summarize a transaction. In other letters, you will request information, often from the custodian of records.

Often you will be responsible for coordinating document productions. Many letters will be written to accompany documents, releases, and checks.

Example:

May 18, 2005

Ms. Rebecca M. Hoffman, Case Manager

American Movies Association

123 Oak Street

Hometown, Virginia 30012

the U.S.A.

Re: Beijing DVD Enterprises Co., Ltd.

Dear Ms. Hoffman,

This letter is to apprise you of the current status of our attempts to trace and locate Beijing DVD Enterprises Co., Ltd.

As you are aware, we have rummaged all available public records and tried to contact the said company through various channels but, unfortunately, it could neither be found nor be traced. We also have checked with relevant local government agencies but could not find any company registered under that name. It appears that Beijing DVD Enterprises Co., Ltd is a fictitious name and has never officially existed.

Therefore, I think the best way to proceed would be to negotiate with Beijing Public Security Bureau (the local police department) as well as local industrial and commerce administration agencies for a criminal investigation into the matter. At the moment, these government organs can at least try to stop further circulation of the pirated copies of your copyrighted movies and sound tracks.

Please do not hesitate to call on me if you have any questions or concerns. I look forward to hearing from you soon.

Sincerely yours,

Mara Cubbon

C. Opinion Letters

Opinion and advice letters advise clients about the legal rules that apply to their situation. Most law firms will not have paralegals draft even a preliminary opinion letter. Always have the supervising attorney review the opinion letter carefully before it is sent to another attorney for signing. An opinion letter must be signed by an attorney because, as its name suggests, the letter states a legal opinion. Many firms require that opinion letters are signed only by partners, as the letter makes the firm responsible for the opinion offered.

We would like to help the client understand how the law applies to his or her particular problem and to explain his or her legal rights and obligations. To give credibility to our conclusions, we need to explain how the law and facts support our reasoning and opinion. Our second purpose, the prescriptive one, is to enable the client to make a decision about how to deal with his or her legal problem. To do so, we must not only set out the options available to the client, but also the risks and benefits of each.

To evaluate each course of action, we must take factors into account, such as expense, delay, risk, emotional conflict, risk, and, of course, the client's specific concerns. It is not our intent to persuade the client or to sway his judgment, but to make sure that he has sufficient understanding of the problem and its possible solutions to make an informed decision about the best means of resolving it.

The following suggestions might be helpful for drafting opinion letters.

1. Begin by addressing your client's question or concern.
2. Summarize the fact upon which your opinion is based.
3. Explain the law and its application.
4. Be objective.
5. Adopt a style and tone appropriate for your reader.

D. Email

Email notes have become very common. Many of the same rules apply in the same way to an e-mail note as they would to any other letters.

Maintain professionalism in e-mails even though the format is considered casual.

Here's a template for each section of a professional email:

> *Subject Line*
> Subject: Your Name—Reason for Writing
>
> *Greeting*
> Dear Mr. /Ms. Last Name,
>
> *Body of Message*
> (Your message should be two or three paragraphs at most and should explain why you're writing and what you're requesting.)
>
> *Closing*
>
> Sincerely,
> Typed Signature and Contact Information
> Mikala Schwartz
> mikala.schwartz@email.com
> 617-123-1234

E. Social Media

Social media, such as Facebook, LinkedIn and X, are now frequently used by many legal professionals. Law firms and corporations rely on social media for marketing and networking. Client and professional correspondence have not yet adopted social media as a form of communication in the law firm environment.

Exercises:

Please find out special considerations for e-mail correspondence.

References:

1. *Consider whether the e-mail is appropriate for this particular communication.*
2. *Be professional.*
3. *Honor the need for client confidentiality.*
4. *Take your time.*

Chapter 14
Writing in Legal Practice

　　实务法律写作的基本类型主要分为两类：向客户提供法律建议的文件通常以办公备忘录的形式，向法院提交的文件通常是以答辩状的形式。本章介绍了上述两类文书的写作方法和技巧。备忘录由几个不同但相关的部分组成，在研究、起草和撰写办公备忘录时，应遵循客观、细致的基本特点。答辩状是律师用于说服法院相信客户的立场是合理的，以及说服法院采纳该立场的正式文件。答辩状在许多方面类似于法律备忘录，适用于备忘录的许多原则也适用于答辩状。但在两个重要方面二者不同。一是文件的语气：答辩状通常采用论证的方式，而备忘录则更加倾向于讨论的方式。二是起草文件时的目标：答辩状以预设基本结论为起点，相比之下，备忘录关注的是如何客观地确定谁的立场最合理，通常要到研究和分析过程的相对后期才会得出结论。

Section 1　The Office Memorandum

　　Legal advice to a client is often based on a formal memorandum of law, which is a basic document of legal writing. Three fundamental principles should guide you in researching, drafting and writing an office memorandum: be objective, be thorough, and communicative.

　　The memorandum is composed of several distinct but related sections. Although there are many variations, the following format for preparing a legal memorandum is widely used.

A. Elements of an Office Memorandum

1. Heading

The heading is the part of memorandum that tells who wrote it, to whom it is written, what it is about, and the date.

Sample:

To: (readers' names and job titles)

From: (your name and job title)

Date: (complete and current date)

Subject: (what the memo is about)

Encl or Attached: other documents which are included with the report (omitted if there are no enclosures).

References: a list of particularly important background documents (omitted if there are no such documents).

2. Questions presented

This section should contain balanced and understandable statements of the legal questions you will answer. The questions presented will parallel the issues that you will analyze in the Discussion section of the memo.

3. Brief answers

This section provides a short answer to each of the questions presented in the preceding section. The brief answer is a conclusion and a brief explanation of the reasons for that conclusion.

4. Statement of facts

The statement of facts is a formal and objective description of the relevant facts in the problem. It must be accurate and complete.

5. Discussion

The discussion is the heart of the memo and is divided into sections according to the issues and sub-issues presented by the problem.

6. Conclusion

The conclusion is longer because it contains a more thorough description of the reasoning supporting the ultimate conclusion. For each issue, it briefly describes the relevant law and explains how the law does or does not apply to the facts in the case at hand.

B. The Discussion

1. State your conclusion on each issue or sub-issue objectively and candidly

Legal memos are written to predict outcomes. Clients rely on memos to make choices about their lives and businesses. Each case is different, and the possible ways to describe your conclusion are limited only by your creativity.

2. Describe the law objectively

Although there are many legitimate ways to describe the law, you must describe it objectively. Objectivity in describing the applicable law is essential to your credibility.

3. Explain the analysis objectively

Objectivity in memorandum writing is important because the weaknesses of your position will come to light sooner or later, and it is better for that to happen sooner.

C. Statement of Facts for a Memorandum

1. Identify the legally significant facts

The legally significant facts are those that will affect the legal outcome of your client's case. You can identify the legally significant facts in a case only after you have identified the relevant rules and the corresponding issues.

2. Identify key background facts

Legally significant facts tell part of the story, but these facts alone may not tell the whole story. Background facts are often needed to make the factual situation understandable and to put the legally significant facts in context.

3. Organize the facts intelligibly

The statement of legally significant and key background facts should tell your client's story completely and coherently. In most cases, the most sensible and convenient method of organization is to relate the facts in chronological order.

4. Describe the facts accurately and objectively

Describe legally significant facts precisely, for they are crucial to the outcome. Be careful to describe the facts rather than evaluate, analyze or characterize them.

D. Questions Presented

1. Be understandable

A question should be as precise and complete as possible without being so complex that your reader cannot understand it. When a legal issue has several sub-issues, you should have a separate question for each.

2. Be objective

An office memo should predict what a court is likely to do with a particular problem. Therefore, you must avoid advocating or anticipating a certain result.

Finally, there is a general sample:

> **OFFICE MEMORANDUM**
>
> TO: ×××, Senior Lawyer
> FROM: ×××, law student
> Client: ×××
> File: document number
> RE: the subject
> Date:
>
> (Main body)
> Present the questions and issues.
> Issues
> (1) Will a court ...
> (2) What will the court ...
> Brief Answer
> Yes/No. There is a reasonable chance ...
> Ideally, the court would ...
> Fact
> Rules Governing the ...
> Discussion
> Courts will ...
> How to ...
> Conclusion

Example(in an age discrimination of employment case)

> **OFFICE MEMORANDUM**
>
> September 12, 2005
> TO: All foreign and domestic summer interns
> FROM: Director of Litigation
> RE: Theory of the Case Memorandum
>
> The defendant employer is liable under the Labor Act for damages, injunctive relief, and attorney's fees for having terminated our client because of his age. Our client will

> make out a prima facie case based on the facts that he was in a protected age category at the time of his termination, was qualified to perform the job, was replaced by a younger person, and was terminated in a workforce reduction that disproportionally impacted persons over 40 years old.
>
> The defendant's effort to establish that our client was unqualified to perform the assigned work will fail to rebut the prima facie case.
>
> In the preceding age discrimination example, this analysis would be as follows.
>
> 1. **Element**: A showing of disparate impact alone establishes a prima facie case of age discrimination.
>
> 2. **Analysis:** In Feihong Group vs. Fort Motors (China), Ltd., the Supreme People's Court held that disparate impact alone establishes a prima facie case of race discrimination, because it raises a permissive inference with regard to the protected class. The same analysis should apply in age discrimination cases, because of congressional intent to create a protected class.
>
> 3. **Known facts:** 12 of 20 persons terminated in the plaintiff's department were over 40 years old.
>
> 4. **Facts to be developed:** age distribution of the defendant's overall work force reduction and remaining workforce.

Exercises:

1. Please explain elements of an Office Memorandum.
2. Please explain steps in discussion part of an Office Memorandum.

Section 2   Brief

The brief is the formal document a lawyer uses both to convince a court that the client's position is sound and to persuade a court to adopt that position. Briefs are similar to office memos in many respects, and many of the principles that apply to memos also apply to briefs.

Briefs differ from memos in two important respects. The first difference is the tone of the documents: brief argue; memos discuss. The second difference is the thinking process used in drafting the documents.

The brief writer knows the basic conclusions in advance. The memorandum writer, by contrast, is concerned with objectively determining whose position is most sound and usually will not come to a conclusion until relatively late in the process of research and analysis.

A. Elements of a Brief

There are two kinds of briefs. Following are generally accepted formats for both the brief to a trial court and the brief to an appellate court (Table 14-1).

Table 14-1 Two Kinds of Briefs

Brief to a Trial Court	Brief to an Appellate Court
Caption	Title Page
	Table of Contents
	Table of Authorities Cited
	Opinion(s) Below
	Constitutional Provisions, Statutes, Regulations, and Rules Involved
	Standard of Review (required by some courts)
Introduction	
Questions Presented (optional)	Questions Presented
Statement of Facts	Statement of Facts
	Summary of Argument
Argument Conclusion	Argument Conclusion
	Appendix(es)

1. Caption or title page

The caption identifies the court, the name of the case, the docket number, the motion or other matter under consideration, the judge, and the side represented.

The title page of an appellate brief is comparable to the caption of a trial court brief. It identified the court, the docket number, the name of the case, the side represented, and the names and addresses of counsel.

2. Table of contents

The table of contents of an appellate brief lists each element of the brief and the page on which that element begins. In addition, the point headings used in the argument should be stated in full in the order they appear, with page numbers corresponding to their locations.

3. Table of authorities cited

This section, sometimes called simply "Table of Authorities" or "Citations," lists all of the legal and other materials used to support the argument in an appellate brief and shows every page on which those materials are cited.

4. Opinions below

This section, also often called "statement of the case", indicates where the decisions of the lower courts or government agencies that have decided this case can be located in case the reviewing court wants to read them.

5. Jurisdiction

This section of an appellate brief, also called a "Jurisdictional Statement" or "Statement of Jurisdiction," provides a short statement of the jurisdictional basis for the appeal.

6. Constitutional provisions, statutes, regulations, and rules involved

This section tells the court what codified provisions are relevant to the determination of the case and where in your brief the judge can scrutinize the exact language of these provisions.

7. Standard of review

This section contains a concise statement of the appropriate standard of review to be exercised by the appellate court, with citations to authority supporting the applicability of that standard.

8. Introduction

Trial court briefs commonly included a short statement identifying the parties and explaining the reason for the brief.

9. Questions presented

This section, sometimes called "issues" or "issues on appeal", states the legal issues involved in a trial or appellate brief and tells the court the matters you intend to address.

10. Statement of facts

The statement of facts in a brief, sometimes also known as "statement of the case" or simply "statement," is a descriptive account of the facts from your client's point of view.

11. Summary of argument

This section of an appellate brief is a concise statement of your major conclusions and the most important reasons supporting them.

12. Argument

The argument is the foundation on which the rest of the brief is constructed. Like the discussion in an office memorandum, it is the heart of the document.

13. Conclusion

This section describes what you want the court to do. It precisely states what relief you are requesting from the court—particularly if the relief you seek is more complicated than affirming or reversing the lower court's judgment.

14. Appendices

This section contains the quoted statutes from the section of your brief called Constitutional Provisions, Statutes, Regulations and Rules involved.

B. Structure of an Argument

1. Present your strongest issues, sub-issue, and argument first.

When your client's case involves several independent issues, present the strongest issue first, followed by the next strongest issue, and the next, and conclude with the weakest.

2. When issues are of equal strength, present the most significant issue first. The most significant issues are not necessarily the strongest ones. The most significant issues are those that, if resolved favorably, would help your client most.

3. Present your client's position on each issue or sub-issue before answering counterarguments.

In a memo, your conclusion may support your client or it may support your opponent. In a brief, however, your conclusion must not only convince the court to decide for your client, it must also convince the court to decide against your opponent.

C. Persuasive Writing

1. Be professional and honest

"A lawyer, as a member of the legal profession, is a representative of clients, an office of the legal system and a public citizen having special responsibility for the quality of justice." Always maintain a professional tone and manner and be honest about the law and the facts.

2. Fully argue your client's position

A legal argument is based on a series of logical or analytical steps that are informative and persuasive only if they are all expressly stated. Please emphasize helpful facts and de-emphasize unhelpful fact, use policy arguments to support your legal analysis.

3. Present arguments from your client's point of view

Emphasize the correctness of your client's position, present the law from your client's point of view, and state your client's position so that it appears objective.

4. Craft sentences and choose words to persuade

The following guidelines are illustrative: Write positive assertions rather than negative ones. Use placement of words, phrases, and sentences to emphasize or minimize points. Use short sentences for emphasis. Be subtle rather than openly manipulative.

D. Point Headings

1. State your legal conclusions and the basic reasons for these conclusions

Point headings should be an integral part of the argument section. They should be confident, forceful so as to be most favorable to your client.

2. Structure point headings to be both specific and readable

Point headings must relate legal rules to specific factual situations. The more specifically these rules and facts are stated, the more persuasive the point headings will be.

3. Place heading at logical points in your brief

Point headings must reflect your organizational scheme. You should outline your brief before drafting it, and the headings you eventually formulate for the argument should correspond to the specific points in your outline.

E. Statement of Facts for a Brief

1. Describe the facts from your client's point of view

Show the court how your client saw the events unfold and describe them in a way that arouses sympathy for your client's position. You should, of course, never omit or distort legally significant facts, whether they help or hurt your position, nor should you include any arguments or argumentative statements.

2. Vividly describe favorable emotional facts and neutralize your opponent's emotional facts.

Facts that are emotionally favorable to your client are valuable persuasive tools when used effectively. The more vividly you describe these facts, the more likely it is that a court will be sympathetic to your client.

3. Organize your statement to emphasize favorable facts and de-emphasize unfavorable facts.

Emphasize, de-emphasize and shade legally and emotionally significant facts by artfully arranging them in the statement of facts. This principle differs from the previous ones in that it concerns location rather than description of specific facts, and it is particularly important when your case involves few emotionally favorable facts.

F. Briefs to a Trial Court

1. Focus more on the applicability of legal rules than on policy

Briefs to trial courts therefore should focus more on the applicable legal rules contained in statutes and cases than on the policy supporting them.

Include the text of any relevant statute and the rules from cases on point, and explain their importance.

2. Emphasize that fairness requires a decision in your client's favor

You should generally focus on the justice of a decision in your client's favor. To the extent possible, you must try to convince the trial judge that your client has behaved prudently and fairly, that the other party has behaved imprudently or unfairly, and that to decide the issue for your client would work justice.

3. Be brief

This principle requires you to make important judgments about what is important enough to include in the brief. If you have cases directly on point, discuss only those. Avoid extended discussions of policy. Keep your argument and analysis as straightforward and simple as possible.

Spend as little time as possible distinguishing the authority relied on by your opponent.

4. Write for the court

Writing for the court involves two considerations—the local court rules and the temperament of the judge. Writing for the court also means tailoring your writing to the interests and temperament of the judge who will decide whether your client wins or loses.

G. Briefs to an Appellate Court

1. Focus on the claimed errors of the lower court

Because an appellate court is responsible for correcting mistakes made by the trial court, you should frame your argument in terms of error you claim the trial court made or error your opponent alleged. The appellate court from the outset must fully appreciate the nature of the error and the procedural context in which it occurred.

2. Base your argument on the appropriate standard of review

Appellate courts exercise different standards of review, depending on the nature of the case and the case's procedural posture when the trial court's decision was issued. The standard of review determines the latitude afforded to the appellate court to substitute its judgment for that of the trial court.

3. Emphasize that a decision in your client's favor would further the policies underlying the law

Appellate briefs should contain a more extensive discussion of policy than trial court briefs. Appellate courts are responsible for providing guidance to the trial courts and for determining the direction of the law within their jurisdictions.

4. Explain how a decision in your client's favor would foster harmony or consistency in the law

Appellate courts are concerned with the orderly development of the law.

They would like to ensure not only that the policies supporting the rules are being served but also that their decision will not create disharmony in the law or set a bad precedent. You must therefore strive to convince the appellate court that a decision in your client's favor is consistent with previous decisions and that it would foster, rather than discourage, a rational development of the law.

Exercise:

Please read the following material and prepare a memo about what options the client has to handle the dispute and the risks relating to the facts.

The client discovered a contract affixed with the official seals of both the client and a company, under which, a company should design, create, and maintain an app account on behalf of the client, and the client should pay RMB 10,000 (VAT inclusive) for the design and creation of the app account and RMB 20,000 (VAT inclusive) for the maintenance of the app account to a company. The client learnt that the contract, which was undated, was signed in around early June, 2020.

The contract also indicated that the period of maintenance was from 1 June, 2020 to 1 June, 2021, and a company should provide certain services during the period of maintenance, including, for example, pushing three to four pieces of news twice per week, providing monthly report for the client and collecting questions raised during interactions and giving feedback to the client.

It was further stated in the contract that, within 5 working days after the execution of the contract, the client should make an up-front payment of an amount equivalent to 60% of the first RMB 10,000 to a company; and within 3 working days after the client's acceptance of the completion of the app account design and creation, the client should pay the remaining 40% of the first RMB 10,000 and 50% of the remaining RMB 20,000 to a company; in October 2020, the client should pay the remaining 50% of the RMB 20,000 to a company; any dispute arising from the contract should be resolved through litigation before a court of a company's locality.

The contract was prepared by a former employee of the client named John Smith. The management of the client was not aware of the contract until the 60% of the first RMB 10,000 was paid to a company. The client then refused to further pay the remaining money under the contract, finding the price of the contract is much higher than the market standard, and sent an email to a company demanding the termination of the contract based on unconscionability on 26 July, 2020. So a company sent an email to the client demanding the outstanding fees. The client and a company had a meeting thereafter, but no settlement was reached.

Chapter 15
Contract Drafting in General

起草合同首先需要了解一份好的合同要达到的目的与效果，了解合同都具有的框架结构，但合同起草不等于将正在起草的合同内容直接填充到固定的框架中。尽管在很多情况下，合同起草要参照其他先例文本中的条款，但这绝不意味着要照搬照抄。起草者必须根据交易的具体情况、当事方的交易目标以及具体指示对有关条款进行起草和修订，在保护当事人利益的同时，保障交易得以按照双方的意愿执行。本章主要介绍一份好的合同应当具有的价值及元素，在起草合同之前应当做的准备，并对合同的主要结构和起草合同的写作技巧做简要概述。

Section 1　Overview of a Good Contract

A good contract should ensure that the parties are able to obtain their intended legal benefits, i.e., remove obstacles to the exercise of their rights.

One of the important aims of lawyers when designing contracts is to reduce the legal risks for their clients, which requires that the advisory letters and contracts produced minimise uncertainty as to the relevant facts or the parties' expressions of intent. This way, if a dispute subsequently arises, it is possible to interpret the legal instruments produced by the lawyer in a manner that is in the interests of the client.

It is worth noting that for parties in economic activity, any legal risk ultimately implies an economic risk, and a legally disadvantaged position usually leads to a financial loss for the party. At the same time, economic risks in the form of legal risks may in some cases even affect the personal rights of the parties, for example, if the parties have committed criminal offences as a result of serious violations of the law in relation to their economic activities. A good legal document is not a purely academic piece of good writing and the writer should always bear in mind when writing a contract that the ultimate goal of the contract is to protect the interests of the parties to the maximum extent in practice.

To do this, two aspects must be considered: On the one hand, whether the contractual provisions themselves may create an obstacle to the parties' obtaining a legitimate interest. On the other hand, whether the legal provisions in question may create obstacles for the parties to exercise their contractual rights. Subsequently, these legal obstacles should be removed as far as possible by adding new contractual provisions or amending existing ones. In the process of drafting the contract, each clause of the contract should be carefully considered and the relationship among the clauses should be rationalized.

A good contract should limit the obligations and responsibilities of the parties to the legal limits agreed upon by both parties. In other words, it is important to avoid subjecting the client to overly onerous obligations and responsibilities.

The contract should be drafted in a way that takes into account the interests of all parties to the transaction, with a view to the successful completion of the transaction and the realization of the interests of the parties. Only if the terms of rights and obligations are more equal, the contract can be signed and performed as soon as possible, enabling the client to achieve its business objectives.

In addition, the range of potential readers of the contract should be taken into account when drafting the contract. Some readers (e.g., judges, arbitrators, government officials) are not part of the project. The lawyer should also consider the range of potential readers who are not directly involved in the project and cannot understand the background of the project. Therefore, the lawyer should try to make the contract as complete and clear as possible. This way, readers who are not parties to the project will be able to understand the content when they read it several years later.

Exercise:

Explain the values behind a good contract.

Section 2   Draft Skills

To draft a good contract, it is usually considered that it should include the following aspects.

The drafter should understand the relevant legal provisions and their practical implementation, and must also master the basic structure of the contract as well as some specific techniques for drafting the contract. Only by understanding the various components of a contract and the relationship between them can a lawyer draft a contract using the relevant specific contractual provisions to most effectively protect the interests of the client.

Contracts must be drafted in a proactive manner to anticipate and prevent risks that may exist during the implementation of the contracted project.

The parties may consider only the current problems they face during the contract negotiation process, without thinking about the problems that may be encountered during the implementation of the project (e.g., one month, one year or two years later). Instead, the attorney should comprehensively assess the risks that may occur during the entire process of contract performance during the contract drafting and negotiation process. At the same time, the lawyer should design practical measures to protect the interests of the client in the event of specific risks and give legal effects to them through contractual provisions.

The drafter should need to understand the common interests of the parties to the contract as well as the divergent interests when drafting the contract, and try to allow both parties to grasp the common interests and deal with the divergent interests in a reasonable manner. A contract must be approved and satisfied by both parties in order to be successfully implemented in practice. Looking out for the interests of the other party does not mean that the interests of one's own client are not protected enough; in fact, understanding and grasping the mindset of the other party is one of the most important protections for one's client. In fact, understanding and grasping the other party's mentality is the most important kind of protection for your client.

The drafter needs to use his or her ability to express the meaning of the parties accurately in writing. When drafting a contract, the basic principle is to fully express the meaning of the parties and to follow the relevant law, and the language should adhere to the tradition of consistency in expression, using short definitive sentences to indicate the meaning of the contract.

Exercise:

Please summarize considerations for contract drafting skills.

Section 3 Preparation Before Drafting a Contract

Before drafting a contract, it is important to first have a clear understanding of the parties' requirements, including the parties' business objectives in this transaction. There are the following issues to consider:

1. What is the client's business objective?
2. How does the client want to achieve this objective?
3. What is the requested "deliverable"?
4. When does the client want the document?
5. How much does the client expect to pay?

The next step is to understand the structure of the entire transaction and the business background, including: whether the parties had similar transactions with each other in the past, and the position of the parties in this transaction. There are the following issues to consider:

1. How many parties?
2. Contractual relationship
3. Legal status, legal relationship, capacity and authority
4. Any prior contracts between parties? Related or unrelated?
5. Any similar prior contracts between the client and other parties?
6. Which party has commercial leverage?
7. How important is this deal for the client?

Subsequently, appropriate legal research should be conducted. According to the principle of freedom of contract, the vast majority of the terms of the contract are agreed upon by the parties, but there are also mandatory and prohibitive legal provisions that can materially affect the rights and obligations of the parties, so it is important to understand these provisions and take countermeasures accordingly.

Finally, consider whether there is a suitable precedent text and how it can be used. The use of precedent texts has two advantages: first, it saves time; second, some of the provisions in the precedent texts are good references and reminders for lawyers drafting contracts for the current transaction, because the issues covered by the precedent texts are likely to reoccur in the current transaction.

After reviewing the precedent text article by article, two related tasks should be done: (1) delete or modify the clauses drafted only for the transaction covered by the precedent text; and (2) add new clauses according to the specific circumstances of the current transaction.

Exercise:

Please list some thoughts for drafting a contract.

Section 4　Structure and Common Types of Contracts

A. Structure

Before drafting a contract, the drafter must first have a clear understanding of the parties' requirements, including the parties' business objectives in this transaction. Under the principle of freedom of contract, the vast majority of the terms of the contract are agreed by the parties, but there are also mandatory, prohibitive legal provisions which can materially affect the rights and obligations of the parties, so it is important that the drafter understands these provisions and responds accordingly. Generally, a contract generally involves that:

1. Offer absolute and unqualified acceptance;
2. Consensus ad idem;
3. Intention to create legal relations;
4. Genuineness of consent
5. Contractual capacity of the parties
6. Legality of object
7. Possibility of performance
8. Certainty of terms
9. Valuable consideration

A typical contract structure consists of the following elements, but this is not a fixed pattern. In the process of drafting a contract, the drafter may use only some of these parts and, depending on some customary practices in different industries, adopt different orders and different levels of detail for each part in the specific drafting process.

1. Preamble
2. Preliminary statements
3. Definitions
4. Operative clauses
5. Conditions precedent
6. Representations and warranties
7. Boilerplate clauses
8. Signature page
9. Schedules and annexes

The above list is a typical contract structure. However, it is not a fixed pattern that is set in stone. Only some parts of it may be used in the process of drafting the contract. Depending on the customary practice in different industries, the order of the parts may vary in the specific drafting of the contract.

The first and second parts of the contract are the initial part and preamble of the contract. The initial part of the contract sets out the nature of the contract and the parties to it, and together with the preamble, provides the relevant background to the contract. The definitions section is a critical part of the entire contract and can be attached to the contract as an appendix. The operating terms are the heart of the contract, and although they take up only a small part of the structure chart, the specific operating terms should actually be the main part of the contract. The specific operating clauses will vary from contract to contract, while the rest of the clauses are relatively stable. The exact location of the conditions precedent and representations and warranties sections in a contract can also vary from contract to contract, and the two sections, conditions precedent and representations and warranties, are not required in all contracts, and lawyers should consider whether they need to be included when drafting a contract. The general terms and conditions section of a contract are usually found in all contracts, but the possibility exists for variations. The signature page is usually at the end of the contract; some contracts have the signature page after the body of the contract and then the appendices and attachments, while some contracts place the signature page at the end of the contract, after the appendices and attachments.

Chinese contract law list general clauses of the contact as: tile or name and domicile of the parties; contract object; quantity; quality; price or remuneration; time limit, place and method of performance; liability for breach of contract; methods to settle disputes.

B. Common Types of Contracts

(1) Nominate contracts in Chinese civil code:

Leasing Contracts

Financial Leasing Contracts

Factoring Contracts

Contracts for Work

Contracts for Construction Projects

(2) Other forms of contracts

Memorandum of Understanding

Letter of Intent

Secrecy Agreement/Agreement of Confidentiality

Collaboration Agreement

Exclusive Distributorship Agreement

Exercise:

Find a contract and suggest improvements based on the contract-drafting standards and framework in this chapter, taking into account the specific content of the contract.

Chapter 16
General Contract Clauses

合同的通用条款是相对于特殊条款而言的，指无论性质如何，通常都会出现的条款。在买卖、合资、租赁、借贷、技术转让等不同类型的合同中，尽管缔约目的不同，但都包括违约责任、免责条款、合同的解除与终止等一般性的约定，这类条款被称为通用条款。合同中的通用条款有时与合同标的或者合同所针对的交易联系不是十分紧密，但通用条款对一份好的合同来说是不可或缺的。

本章以合同结构为顺序介绍常见的通用条款，一般而言，通用条款包括定义及解释条款、完整协议与可分割性条款、违约条款、声明及保证条款、保密条款、转让条款、知识产权条款、赔偿条款、税收条款、期限与终止条款、保险条款、不可抗力条款、管辖法律与争议解决条款、责任及义务条款。

Section 1 Cover

The cover of a contact is composed of confidential mark, title, signature parties and date. The sample is listed as follows.

Confidential
Transaction Documents
Date/Month/Year

CONCESSION AGREEMENT
for the construction, installation, financing, management, improvement, expansion operation, maintenance, rehabilitation, repair and refurbishment of the nationwide transmission and sub-transmission system in the Republic of the XXX

> Among
>
> *XXX Corporation*
>
> And
>
> *XXX Corporation*
>
> *[CONCESSIONAIRE]*
>
> *[date]*

Exercise:

Please summarize key elements of a contract cover.

Section 2 Commencement, Whereas and Transition

A. Commencement

The commencement of a contract generally includes: the corporate or personal names of the parties to the contract and their nationalities, principle places of business or residential addresses, the date and place of signing the contract.

This contract/agreement (is)made/entered into/concluded in place on the day of month, year, by and between/among party names, a company/corporation duly organized/incorporated (and existing) under the law of state, country with its legal address/registered office/domicile at address (hereinafter referred to as party A), ...

Examples:

This contract, made and entered into the 10th day of May, 2013, by and
between Baiweilin, a corporation duly organized and existing under the
laws of People's Republic of China with its domicile at Shanghai
(hereinafter referred to as Party A), and Unilever, a company incorporated
and existing under the laws of Britain with its domicile at
London (hereinafter referred to as Party B).

This operation and maintenance contract, made this _____ day of _____,
2014, by and between ABC Power Generation Company Limited, a Sino
foreign cooperative joint venture ("owner"), and XYZ Power Generation
Corporation, a Chinese company ("Operator").

B. Whereas Clause

The main contents of the whereas clause generally include: an explanation of the purpose of the contract, a description of the background facts that led to the agreement of the parties, and a determination of a uniform understanding of the important elements of the contract, etc.

Whereas clause is not a required term of a contract, so if the transaction itself does not have a unique context, there is no need to include a whereas clause in the contract. The whereas clause should be concise and avoid the terminology used in the contract should be brief, avoiding too much background on the project, and should avoid defining terms that will appear in specific operating terms. The terminology used should be defined. This does not mean, however, that no terms should be defined in the whereas clause. For example, if other contracts and transactions are involved when presenting the background, they can be usually defined in the whereas clause.

Whereas,

Party A has the right of

is a corporation engaged to

desires/wishes/agrees to

Party A desires to/wishes to/will

Party B agrees to/has agreed to

Examples:

Whereas, this agreement is supplemental to an agreement dated 9 December, 2009 between the parties to this agreement ("the Principal Agreement") under which the purchaser agreed to buy certain assets of the vendor for an aggregate sum of $3 million.

Whereas,

Manufacturer is engaged in the manufacture and sale of the products;

Manufacturer is desire to sell the products in the territory.

C. Transition Clause

The purpose of this section is to carry on from the top, indicating that the specific terms of the contract follow here.

Now therefore, in consideration of:

the premise herein,

the payment to be made by _____ to _____,

the forgoing,

The parties to this agreement hereby agree as follows:

Now, therefore, in consideration of the foregoing, and for other good and valuable consideration, the receipt and sufficiency of which is hereby acknowledged, the parties hereto covenant and agree as follows:

Example:

Therefore, in consideration of the premises and the mutual conveniences, the Licensee and the Licensor, through consultation, agree to enter into this contract under the terms and conditions set forth as follows.

Exercise:

Please explain the functions of whereas clause and transition clause.

Section 3 Definition, Interpretation and Validity

A. Definition and Interpretation

The purpose of definitions and interpretations is to unify the understanding of the relevant concepts in the terms and conditions, to improve the efficiency of the text, and to provide explanations for resolving problems after disputes have arisen. The explanation can be included as a clause at the beginning of the contract or in an annex.

Methods of definition and interpretation:

1. Agree on specific terms;
2. Cite the description of a specific term in other documents and laws;
3. No operative provisions in definitions;
4. Avoid circular definitions;
5. Do not need to define terms if "ordinary meaning" is sufficient;
6. Use defined terms consistently throughout the contract.

Definition. In this agreement, the following terms shall have the following meanings unless the context clearly requires otherwise:

TERM, means

    refers to

    shall have the same meaning defined in

    shall be construed as

    incluedes

In relation to   TERM,

For the purpose of

In connection with

In respect of

It means/refers to/shall be construed as ...

Examples:

In this contract, "person" means

(i) a natural person and any corporation or other entities which is given, or is recognized as having, legal personality by the law of any country or territory; or

(ii) any unincorporated association or unincorporated body of persons, whether formed in the United States or elsewhere, including a partnership.

"Business Day" means a day on which banks and foreign exchange markets are open for business in the People's Republic of China and Britain.

"Proceedings" means any proceedings before a court or tribunal (including an arbitration), whether in the People's Republic of China or elsewhere.

B. Validity

This part deals with the basic conditions for the entry into force of the contract and is of legal importance. The content of the contractual effect consists of two main groups of clauses, usually placed at the beginning and end of the contract, respectively, as a preamble clause and a closing clause.

1. Preamble clause

The first group of clauses is written at the beginning of the contract, mainly concerning the qualification and capacity of the parties, mainly including.

(1) the names and legal addresses of the parties to the contract: the names of the parties to the contract must be written in full when they first appear in the contract, and can be abbreviated when repeated later, abbreviated as Party A or Party B, the Buyer or Seller, the Licensor or Licensee (hereinafter referred to as Party A or Party B; the Buyer or the Seller; the Licensor or Licensee), etc.

Legal address, primarily the place of business, domicile, or residence.

(2) Date and place of contracting: the date and place of contracting relate to the applicable law in the event of a dispute over the contract.

(3) The legal relationship between the parties to the contract, requiring an indication of who is the buyer and who is the seller, or the transferor, transferee, lender or borrower, etc.

Example:

This contract is made this 17th date of Oct., 2013 in Beijing, China by and between ABC (Full Name) Company under the law of _____, having its registered address in _____. Its legal address is _____ (hereinafter referred to as the "Buyer") and DEF (Full Name)

Company under the law of _____, having its registered address in _____ (hereinafter referred to as the "Seller"); where the Buyer agrees to buy and the Seller agrees to sell the following goods on terms and conditions as below.

2. Concluding clause

The second group of clauses is written at the end of the contract and its main contents are: the language used in the contract, the number of copies of the contract, the validity of the various texts, the effective time of the contract, the effect of amendments and additions to the contract, the signatures of the parties, etc.

If the contract includes an annex, it should also be stipulated in the contract on the validity of the annex, for example: "The annex shall form an integral part of this contract." (The annex shall be an integral part of this contract.) In addition, this part may also contain a clause on the severability of the contract.

Example (Language Clause)

This contract is made out in duplicate in Chinese and in English language, one Chinese original copy and one English original copy for each party, both texts being equally authentic.

If there is any discrepancy between the Chinese version and English version in this contract, the Chinese version shall prevail.

Any amendment to this contract will be valid only after the authorized representatives of both parties have signed written documents, forming integral parts of the contract.

Example: (Severability Clause)

If any provision of this agreement is determined to be invalid, illegal or unenforceable, the remaining provisions of this agreement remain in full force, if the essential terms and conditions of this agreement for each party remain valid, binding and enforceable.

Exercise:

Please explain the influence of language clause in a contract.

Section 4　Assignment, Indemnification and Warranty

A. Assignment Clause

An assignment clause of a contract is the transfer of all or part of the rights and obligations of the contract by one of the parties to a third party. The third party is the assignee of the contract.

Assignment clauses typically include

1. General provisions as to whether each party has the right to assign and whether the prior consent of the other party must be obtained.

2. The notification obligations of the assigning party.

3. The obligation of the notified party to respond.

4. The right of the first refusal of the other party.

5. The performance obligations of the assignee.

Example:

Neither party may assign, directly or indirectly, all or part of its rights or obligations under this agreement without the prior written consent of the other party.

B. Indemnification and Warranty

The purpose of representations and warranties is for one party in a contract to make representations about information that is in its possession and that is not available or difficult for the other party to obtain, and to warrant to the other party that the representations are true. Usually, representations and warranties relate to facts that are relevant to the party making the representation and are difficult for the other party to determine the truth or falsity.

The significance of representations and warranties to the other party is that the other party agrees to sign and execute this contract based on the representations and warranties made by the representing party as to certain facts. If, in the course of the contract, the other party discovers that these representations and warranties are untrue, it can use this as a basis for the measures for which it seeks relief, such as rescission or termination of the contract, or a claim for compensation.

The warranties agreed in the contract generally refer to guarantee of quality, guarantee of right and guarantee of performance.

Example:

Representations and Warranties

1. Representation of Both Parties. Each of the parties represents and warrants to the other party as follows:

    (a) Organization and Authority. It is a corporation duly organized and validly existing under applicable laws, and has all requisite corporate power and authority to carry on its business as now being conducted, to execute and deliver

this agreement, and to consummate the transactions contemplated hereby.

(b) Authorization ...

Exercise:

Please explain the functions of indemnification and warranty clauses.

Section 5   Rescission and Termination Clause

Dissolution of a contract is a legal act in which one of the parties notifies the other party of the dissolution of the original contractual legal relationship due to the occurrence of subjective and objective circumstances that make the performance of the contract unnecessary or impossible before the contract is performed or not fully performed. Once the contract is dissolved, neither party has the right to request the other party to continue the performance.

In Chinese Civil Code, Article 563 provides that parties may rescind the contract under any of the following circumstances:

(1) the purpose of a contract is not able to be achieved due to force majeure;

(2) prior to expiration of the period of performance, one of the parties explicitly expresses or indicates by his act that he will not perform the principal obligation;

(3) one of the parties delays his performance of the principal obligation and still fails to perform it within a reasonable period of time after being demanded;

(4) one of the parties delays his performance of the obligation or has otherwise acted in breach of the contract, thus makes it impossible for the purpose of the contract to be achieved; or

(5) any other circumstance as provided by law.

The termination of a contract is based on the legal fact that the contractual legal relationship is extinguished due to the completion of the performance of the contract, an arbitration award or a court judgment, or the consent of the parties to the contract.

Factors may result in termination of a contract:

1. Stipulated by the contract itself

2. Breach of the contract

3. Interrupted by unforeseeable situation

4. Term: The parties agree that this contract will be valid for 5 years as of the date of signature of the parties.

In Chinese Civil Code, Article 557 provides that a claim or obligation shall be terminated under any of the following circumstances:

(1) the obligation has been performed;

(2) the obligations are offset against each other;

(3) the debtor has placed the subject matter in escrow in accordance with law;

(4) the creditor has exempted the obligation;

(5) the claim and obligation are merged to be held by the same person; or

(6) any other circumstance under which the parties' agreement is terminated as provided by law or agreed by the parties.

The relationship of rights and obligations under a contract shall be terminated upon rescission of the contract.

Under certain conditions, the termination of the contract does not affect the survival of other rights agreed upon by the parties.

For example:

After the termination of the contract, Party A still has the right to use the know-how supplied by Party B, and still have the right to design, manufacture, use, sell and export the contract product.

Exercise:

Please explain the legal effect of contract termination.

Section 6　Default Clause

Breach of the contract can lead to consequences of a different nature, and the remedies available to the damaged party are therefore different. The nature of the default is generally divided into three kinds of minor default, major default, fundamental default.

Usually, when one party is in material breach of the contract, the damaged party will pursue the other party's liability for breach of the contract through litigation and arbitration. In contract drafting, it is common to refer to the concept of "breach of the contract" in general terms, which can enumerate some of the circumstances that are considered to be a material breach.

A "fundamental breach" applies when no practical remedy exists after the breach has occurred, and the damaged party can exercise its right to terminate the contract as soon as the defaulting party has committed what is considered to be a fundamental breach, without prior notice of breach or notice of termination with extension of time. If a party fails to perform the contract or its performance of the contractual obligations does not conform to the agreed terms and thereby causes damage to the other party, the amount of damage compensation shall be equivalent to the damages caused by the breach of the contract.

Example:

Should either Party A or Party B fails to pay on schedule the contributions in accordance with the provisions defined in Chapter Six to this contract, the defaulting party shall pay to the other party 10% of the contribution starting from the first month after exceeding the time limit.

Where the supplier fails to deliver any or all the goods within the period specified in the contract, the purchaser shall deduct from the contract price of 3% as penal sum and continue to perform its obligations specified in the contract.

Exercise:

Please discuss considerations in drafing default clause.

Section 7 Dispute Settlement Clause

Generally, in the dispute resolution clause in a contract, the parties generally agree to first negotiate amicably and, if negotiation fails, to arbitrate in accordance with an arbitration clause or supplementary arbitration agreement, or, if there is no arbitration clause and there is no supplementary arbitration agreement after a dispute has arisen, to choose litigation as the solution. Under certain conditions, the parties may agree on the competent court and may also agree on the applicable law.

A. Arbitration

After a contractual dispute has arisen, if the parties have an arbitration clause in the contract or have negotiated an arbitration agreement before or after the dispute has arisen, any party to the contract may request, as a claimant, that the agreed arbitration committee decide the contractual dispute between them. An arbitration clause should be drawn up with the following in mind.

1. There is an arbitration agreement. The arbitration agreement is the primary basis for the parties' application and the source of the power of the arbitral institution to arbitrate.

2. There is a specific request for arbitration and facts and reasons for the appointment of a specific arbitral institution.

For Example:

To resolve the disputes through friendly consultation or a third party mediation.

All disputes arising from the execution of, or in connection with the contract shall be settled through friendly negotiation between both parties. In case no settlement to disputes can be reached through negotiation, the disputes shall be submitted for arbitration.

All disputes arising from the execution of, or in connection with this contract shall be settled through friendly negotiation between both parties. In case no settlement to disputes can be reached through friendly negotiation, the disputes shall be submitted to the China International Economic and Trade Arbitration Commission for arbitration in accordance with the Arbitration Rules and the Procedure for the said Commission.

The arbitration award shall be final and binding upon both contracting parties. Neither party shall seek recourse from a court for revising the decision.

B. Governing Law

Contracts usually agree on the rights, obligations and material matters of direct relevance to the parties to the extent possible to be predetermined. Other issues may be designated in the contract to be interpreted by the statute of a particular country, and such a clause designating the statute of a particular country is known as a governing law clause. The governing law of the contract is the law chosen or designated by the parties to apply to the contract or the standard law deemed most appropriate to control the particular point in dispute.

The essence of the governing law clause is the parties' choice of law, i.e., the interpretation of the validity, time of formation, content and interpretation of the contract, performance of the contract, liability for breach of contract, as well as the modification, suspension, assignment, discharge and termination of the contract, or the question of which country or place of law is applicable in the event of a dispute among the parties in this regard.

This contract shall be governed by and construed in accordance with the law of _____.

In any action between any of the parties arising out of or relating to this agreement or any of the transaction contemplated by this contract, each of the parties irrevocably and unconditionally consents and submits to the exclusive jurisdiction and venue of _____ court located in _____.

The parties to a contract involving foreign interests may choose the proper law applicable to the settlement of contract disputes, unless otherwise stipulated in the law.

The signing, validity, interpretation, execution, amendments, termination and arbitration to this Contract shall be governed by the laws of _____.

Example:

The laws of the People's Republic of China shall apply to contracts for Sino-foreign joint venture, Sino-foreign contractual joint venture and Sino-foreign cooperative exploration and development of natural resources, which are performed within the territory of the People's Republic of China.

Exercise:

Please clarify the relationship between dispute resolution clause and governing law clause.

Section 8　Force Majeure Clause

As a result of the event that one party could not have foreseen at the time of conclusion of the contract, being unable to either avoid or overcome its occurrence and consequences.

If a contract cannot be performed owing to force majeure, all or part of the obligations shall be relieved, depending on the impact of force majeure, unless otherwise stipulated in the laws. If force majeure occurs after a party delays the performance, it shall not be relieved of its obligations.

Drafting the exemption clause (force majeure clause), the following issues should be noted.

1. The scope and type of force majeure should be clearly agreed.

2. It should be agreed that after the occurrence of force majeure, the responsible party shall notify the other party of the manner, the time limit and the manner of issuing the documents proving the force majeure event.

3. Determine the legal consequences affected or caused by the force majeure event.

There are two types of legal consequences arising from force majeure events: One is that both parties negotiate to extend the period of performance of the contract and the other is that both parties negotiate to decide whether to cancel the contract.

Example:

The seller shall not be responsible for the delay of shipment or non-shipment in the following events of Force Majeure, including fires, floods, earthquakes, tsunamis, wars, strikes and blockade.

Both parties shall, through consultations, decide whether to terminate the contract or to exempt the part of obligations for implementation of the contract or whether to delay the execution of the contract according to the effects of the events of Force Majeure on the performance of the contract.

Exercise:

Please explain the legal effect of force majeure clause.

Section 9 Miscellaneous

In addition to the various general terms described above, there is often a miscellaneous clause (miscellaneous) at the end of contract, also known as other terms, to some of the simpler terms together. Common are notice, waiver and so on. The language and severability provisions described earlier are sometimes placed at the end of the contract as part of the miscellaneous provisions.

Example (Notice)

All notices required or permitted by this agreement shall be in writing and shall be deemed sufficient where sent by the certified mail to the receiving party at the address set forth above or at such other addresses as that party may have designated in writing.

Example (No Waiver)

No waiver of any term, provision or condition of this agreement, the breach or default thereof, shall be deemed to be either a continuing waiver or a waiver of a subsequent breach or default of any such term, provision or condition of this agreement.

Exercises:

Please indicate the category of each of the following contractual terms.

1. *The validity, interpretation and implementation of this contract shall be governed by the laws of [the People's Republic of China][another jurisdiction] (without regard to its rules governing conflict of laws).*
2. *Failure or delay on the part of any of the parties hereto to exercise a right under this contract shall not operate as a waiver thereof, nor shall any single or partial exercise of such a right preclude any other future exercise thereof.*
3. *This contract may not be assigned in whole or in part by the party without the prior written consent of the other party hereto.*

Chapter 17
Special Contract Clauses

合同的类型和种类有非常大的差异，除了一般的合同条款，对于部分类型的合同而言，特殊合同条款对达到合同目的有至关重要的作用。对于一些特殊的合同条款形式，需要注意法律规定。本章选取保密条款、保险条款、竞业禁止条款、风险转移条款和格式条款等比较常见的特殊条款做简要介绍。

In addition to general contractual terms, contractual terms that are important to the type of contract, or that are specifically provided for in the law, will appear in different types of contracts. This chapter will list some of the more common special contract clauses.

Section 1　Confidentiality Clause

Based on the protection of trade secrets, the provisions of confidentiality clauses are commonly found in contracts relating to intellectual property, technical services and often pay special attention to. Broadly speaking, confidentiality includes two aspects: non-disclosure (to keep the disclosed information confidential) and non-abuse (not to use the disclosed information other than in connection with the agreement). Depending on the circumstances, the parties to the contract may negotiate the scope of the confidentiality content or agree on the duration of confidentiality.

It should be cared that the confidentiality clause is not too demanding to obstacle the performance of the contract. Exceptions to confidential information may include:

(1) information that a party discloses to a court in compliance with an order issued by a court;

(2) information provided by the disclosing party to the government administrative authorities in response to mandatory provisions of the law; and

(3) information publicly disclosed by a listed company in response to mandatory

provisions of the stock exchange for the disclosure of its information.

Examples:

The existence of this contract, as well as its content, shall be held in confidence by both parties and only disclosed as may be agreed to by both parties or as may be required to meet securities disclosure or export permit requirements. Neither party shall make public statements or issue publicity or media releases with regard to this contract or the relationship between the parties without the prior written approval of the other Party.

From time to time prior to and during the term of this contract either party ("disclosing party") has disclosed or may disclose confidential information to the other party ("Receiving Party"). The receiving party shall, during the term of this contract and for two years thereafter:

(a) maintain the confidentiality of confidential information;

(b) not to use confidential information for any purpose other than those specifically set out in this contract; and

(c) not disclose any such confidential information to any person or entity, except to its employees or employees of its affiliates, its agents, attorneys, accountants and other advisors who need to know such information to perform their responsibilities and who has signed written confidentiality contracts containing terms at least as stringent as the terms provided in this article.

Exercise:

Please try to explain the scope of confidential clause.

Section 2　Insurance Clause

In the modern business world, insurance plays an important role, which involves the interests of both buyers and sellers. It is also frequently used in contracts, especially in international trade contracts.

Generally, the insurance clauses involve the insurance amount, the insured class, the insurance premium, the insurance documents and the applicable insurance terms. The parties to the contract can agree on the insurance terms by themselves according to the will of both parties, and can also apply the international common trade terms.

Examples:

1. Covering all risks for 110% of the invoice value as per insurance: Policy of People's

Insurance Company of China (P.I.C.C.) To be affected by the Buyer.
2. Insurance to be covered by the Sellers for 110% of the invoice value against All Risks and War Risks as per Ocean Marine Cargo Clauses of the People's Insurance Company of China dated Jan.1, 2012.

Section 3   Anti-Competition Clause

Anti-competition clauses are often set in service contracts, such as employment contracts, agency contracts and service agreements. The purpose is to protect their trade secrets or core technologies. This part is sometimes reflected as a separate anti-competition agreement.

In general, there are two types of anti-competition clauses: One is to ensure that a party who has acquired a specific position as a result of a contract cannot threaten the special position of another party. This is the case with employment contracts and employment agreements. The second type of restriction is the one that prevents the party who has lost a particular status by contract from engaging in activities that threaten the status of the party who has acquired it by contract.

Usually, the restrictions in the clause cover time, territory, and field, and the clause may also agree on compensation and penalty, etc.

Example:

In further consideration of employment, the employee shall not engage in a business in any manner similar to, or in competition with, the company's or the company's affiliated businesses during the term of his or her employment. Furthermore, the employee shall not engage in a business in any manner similar to or in competition with the company's business for a period of _____ (___) years from the date of termination of his or her employment with the company in the geographical area within a _____ (___) mile radius of any present or future office opened by the company during the term of employment and the geographical area within a _____ (___) mile radius of the employee's home address.

The Party B agrees that it will not during this agreement or for a period of two years after the termination of this agreement be involved whether as principal, partner, agent, contractor or employer in the manufacture, sale or distribution in the territory of any products which the Party B has distributed under this Agreement.

Exercise:

Please explain the background for the rise of anti-competition clause.

Section 4　Risk and Title Passing Clause

In a contract of sale or other contract with delivery of the subject matter, the transfer of risk and title clause is crucial. The parties may agree on the retention of ownership or separately on the assumption of the risk of loss of the subject matter. In the absence of mutual agreement of the parties, it is as provided by law.

As a convention that extensively regulates international trade transport, the United Nations Convention on Contracts for the International Sale of Goods (hereinafter referred to as CISG) is often used as the first rule that the parties to an international trade contract choose to apply. With regard to the transfer of title, Articles 31 to 34 of CISG provide relevant rules on delivery of the goods and handing over of documents; Articles 66 to 70 of CISG provides relevant rules on passing of risk. These two parts are interrelated. In a contract of sale, risk passes when the seller performs its obligations.

Article 67 of CISG provides that when the contract of sale involves the carriage of goods and the seller is not required to deliver at a particular place, the risk passes to the buyer from the moment the goods are delivered to the first carrier in the manner agreed in the contract.

Article 68 of CISG regulates transactions with goods in transit, where the time of signing of the contract between the buyer and seller is considered to be the time of transfer of risk. However, the time of passing of risk varies slightly depending on the circumstances, e.g. the time of passing of risk may be determined, depending on the needs of the parties, as from the time of delivery of the goods. Article 68 also provides that if the seller knows that the goods have been damaged, i.e. are in a situation where they cannot be delivered in full, and deliberately conceals this, the risk is transferred to the seller.

The Chinese Civil Code also has relevant provisions on the burden of risk.

1. Provisions on the burden of risk in case of delay in delivery of the subject matter.

Article 605 provides that where a subject matter fails to be delivered within the agreed time limit because of the buyer, the buyer shall bear the risk of damage to or loss of the subject matter as from the date it breaches the agreement.

2. The burden of risk in the event that the buyer does not receive the subject matter.

Article 609 provides that where the seller has placed the subject matter at the place of delivery in accordance with the agreement or in accordance with the provisions of

Paragraph 2(2), Article 603 of this Code, while the buyer fails to take delivery in breach of the agreement, the risk of damage to or loss of the subject matter shall pass to the buyer on the date of breach of the agreement.

3. Failure to deliver documents and information does not affect the transfer of risk.

Article 609 provides that the failure of the seller to deliver the documents and information relating to the subject matter as agreed upon shall not affect the passing of the risk of damage to or loss of the subject matter.

In the process of drafting a contract, when drawing up provisions relating to the transfer of risk, the drafter should take care to be consistent with the applicable legal provisions.

Example (Retention of title)

If the parties have validly agreed on retention of title, the goods shall remain the property of the seller until the complete payment of the price, or as otherwise agreed.

Example (Transfer of risk)

The seller hereby assumes all risk of loss, damage or destruction resulting from fire or other casualty to the time of transfer of assets and closing.

Exercise:

Please compare transfer of risk in sales of goods from provisions of Chinese law and CISG.

Section 5 Standard Terms

Sometimes contract need to be prepared by one party, to be signed by another party in a weaker position. It is called a standard-form contract. Standard terms are clauses that is pre-drafted by the parties for repeated use and is not negotiated with the other party at the time of contract formation.

Compared with ordinary clauses, standard terms have obvious advantages, such as they can reduce transaction costs, improve transaction efficiency, clearly allocate risks and enhance transaction security. However, at the same time, there are also defects that cannot be ignored, such as limiting the principle of freedom of contract, leading to different allocation of risks in the contract, and harming the interests of disadvantaged counterparties due to the unequal contracting status of the parties.

Therefore, in the Chinese Civil Code, there are stricter regulations on standard terms than general clauses.

On the procedure for the conclusion of standard terms, Article 496 provides that where standard terms are adopted for contracting, the party furnishing the standard terms shall define the rights and obligations between the parties under the principle of fairness, remind in a reasonable manner the other party to note the terms excluding or limiting the liability of the party furnishing the standard terms or otherwise related to the material interest of the other party, and explain the terms upon request of the other party. If the party furnishing the standard terms fails to perform the reminding or explanation obligation, resulting in the other party failing to note or understand the terms in which it has a material interest, the other party may argue that the terms are not a part of the contract.

On the effectiveness of standard terms, Article 496 provides that the following situations will lead to the invalidity of the form clause:

(1) The party furnishing the standard clauses unreasonably excludes or limits its liability, aggravates the liability of the other party, or restricts the main rights of the other party.

(2) The party furnishing the standard clauses excludes the main rights of the other party.

On the interpretation of standard terms, three principles should be followed:

(1) It should be interpreted according to the common understanding. In other words, the standard terms should be interpreted in accordance with the average and reasonable understanding of the possible contracting parties.

(2) The clauses should be interpreted unfavorably to the party providing them.

(3) Non-standard terms take precedence over standard terms. If in a contract, there are both standard terms and non-standard terms (i.e., the clauses drawn up by mutual agreement of the parties), and the content of the two terms is inconsistent, then the use of different terms will have a significant and different impact on the interests of both parties. In this case, according to the principle of non-standard terms, terms should be used, which also fully respects the meaning of the parties, and in general is also more conducive to the protection of the majority of consumers.

Exercises:

1. When drawing up a standard-form contract, in what way can the signing party be explicitly reminded of reasonable care?
2. Assume a situation where a sale contract needs to be drawn up, with the transfer of title and assumption of risk clauses from the perspective of the buyer and the seller respectively.

Appendix
Legal Vocabulary

Section 1   Common Latin Words

These Latin words are not commonly used in writing. This section listed the words and its English meaning for readers to look up when presented in the reading.

Latin Words—English meaning

1. ab initio—from the beginning
2. ad hoc—for this purpose
3. ad litem—for the lawsuit
4. alibi—elsewhere (a defense that the accused was elsewhere when the offense was committed)
5. amicus curiae—friend of the court
6. arguendo—for purpose of argument
7. bona fide—good faith
8. caveat emptor—let the buyer beware
9. casus belli—an act justifying war
10. caveat—a warning
11. contra proferentem—against the one who offers
12. damnun absque injuria—a loss without a wrong
13. de minimis non curat lex—the law does not concern itself with insignificant matters
14. de novo—anew
15. cjusdem gencris—of the same class
16. cxabundanti cautela—from an excess of caution
17. et al—and others

18. ex parte—from one side

19. expressio unius est exclusio—the express mention of one is the exclusion of another

20. ex post facto—after the fact

21. flagrante delicto—in the commission of the offense

22. forum non conveniens—inconvenient forum

23. generalia specialibus non derogant—general words do not derogate from special words

24. habeas corpus—you have the body

25. in haec verba—in these words

26. in pari materia—in equivalent material

27. in propria persona—in his own proper person

28. in re—in the matter of

29. inter alia—among others

30. lex fori—the law of the forum

31. lex loci—the law of the place

32. mala fides—bad faith

33. mutatis nulandis—all necessary changes having been made

34. nil—nothing

35. non compos mentis—not of sound mind

36. non obstante verdicto—notwithstanding the verdict

37. non scquitur—it does not follow

38. noscitur a socils—it is known from its associates

39. nunc pro tunc—now for then

40. pari passu—with equal step

41. per capita—by heads

42. per curiam—by the court (said of a decision not identifying the judge who wrote it)

43. per se—by itself

44. per stirpes—by roots (said of the division of property)

45. prima facie—at first appearance

46. pro rata—in proportion

47. pro tem (pro tempore)—for the time being

48. quid pro quo—something for something

49. respondeat superior—let the superior answer (the employer is liable for the acts of

his employees)

    50. quorum—of whom (the minimum number of people required for a meeting)

    51. reddendo singula singulis—rendering each to each

    52. scienter—having knowledge

    53. scintilla—little spark (said of the tiniest particle of evidence or proof)

    54. scriatim—one after the another

    55. sine qua non—without which it could not be

    56. situs—location

    57. stare decisis—to stand by the decided matters (precedents must be followed)

    58. sui generis—of its own kind

    59. sua sponte—of one's own will

    60. ultra vires—beyond the power

    61. vel non—or not

    62. versus—against

Section 2   Common Legal Terms in Case Reading

In case reading, there exist legal terms and abbreviated terms with particular meaning. This section provides the interpretation of common legal terms in civil and criminal litigation to help readers have better understanding. Meanwhile, this section explains the meaning of abbreviated terms that often appeared in cases to help readers cite and analyze cases more conveniently.

A. Common Legal Terms in Civil Litigation

1. damage: loss, injury, or deterioration, caused by the negligence, design, or accident of one person to another related to a person or property.

2. damages: It generally means an award of money, paid by the wrongdoer, to compensate the victim. There are many kinds of damages, including: (1) actual damages: It refers to the real, substantial and just damages, or the compensation for actual and real loss or injury. (2) consequential damages: The loss or injury is not caused directly and immediately by the wrong act, but from the consequences of wrong act. (3) direct damages: It follows immediately upon the act, or arises naturally or predictably in an ordinary course of human experience. (4) punitive damages: Punitive damages are awarded against a wrongdoer to punish him for his outrageous conduct. Punitive damages are based on different public

policy consideration. (5) incidental damages: A term used by the Uniform Commercial Code, including commercially reasonable charges, expenses or commissions incurred in stopping delivery and in the transportation, care and custody of goods after the buyer's breach, in connection with the return or resale of the goods or otherwise resulting from the breach.

3. joint and several liability: When two or more persons are jointly and severally liable, they are legally responsible together and individually. Each wrongdoer is responsible for the entire judgment.

4. forum: It refers to a court or judicial tribunal that has jurisdiction to hear a lawsuit or petition, or to give remedy where pursued. It relates to several important terms that include: (1) forum actus: The forum of the place where the act was done. (2) forum contractus: The court of the place where a contract is made. (3) forum domicili: The court of the domicile of a defendant. (4) forum conveniens: The state or judicial district in which an action may be most appropriately brought, considering the best interest of the parties and the public. (5) forum non conveniens: The term refers to discretionary power of a court to decline jurisdiction when convenience of parties and ends of justice would be better served if action were brought and tried in another forum. (6) forum shopping: It occurs when a party attempts to have his action tried in a particular court or jurisdiction where he hopes to receive the most favorable judgment or verdict.

5. complaint: It is the first pleading document filed with the court by a party claiming legal rights against another. The party filing the complaint is called the plaintiff and the party against whom the complaint is called the defendant. A complaint usually contains a short and plain statement of the grounds on which the court's jurisdiction depends, the factual and legal claims, and a demand for judgment for the relief.

6. cause of action: It refers to a legal claim recognized and enforceable by law that a plaintiff pleads or alleges in a complaint to start a lawsuit. It is the basis of a lawsuit.

7. tort: It refers to a private or civil wrong or injury, which is a violation of certain duty owed to the plaintiff. Such duty generally arise by operation of law and not by mere agreement of parties.

8. negligence: It refers to the commission of something that a reasonable and prudent man would not do, or the omission of something that a reasonable man guided by ordinary considerations would do.

9. issue of law: It refers to an issue in a lawsuit that relates to determining what the law is, how it should be applied to the facts, and other pure legal points. Issue of law is decided

by judge, not the jury.

10. issue of fact: It refers to an issue involving the resolution of a factual dispute and within the province of jury.

11. ad damnum: It means "to the damage". It is a technical clause used in writs and complaints which states the plaintiff's money loss or the damages claimed.

12. service of process: The delivery of copies of legal documents, such as summons, complaint, and subpoena.

13. summons: An instrument used to commence an action and a mean to acquire jurisdiction over a defendant. It is the formal notice from the court ordering the defendant to appear.

14. affidavit: A written testimony or statement of facts, made voluntarily and out of court, sworn to be true under the oath before a notary public. The person who makes and subscribes an affidavit is called affiant.

15. statute of limitations: It is the statutory period within which a lawsuit must be commenced. If the lawsuit or claim is not filed before the deadline, the right to make a claim is barred. In certain situation, the statue of limitations can be extended due tot the delay in discovering the injury.

16. jurisdiction: The authority and power of a court to hear and determine a judicial proceeding. (1) *in personam* jurisdiction or personal jurisdiction: It is the power that a court has over the defendant's person and that is required before a court can enter an *in personam* judgment; (2) *in rem* jurisdiction: It is the power of a court over a thing that allows the court to dispose of a property within its geographical limits in an action over the thing; (3) territorial jurisdiction: The court's jurisdiction is limited to cases arising or persons residing within a defined territory, such as a state.

17. motion: It refers to a written or oral application made to the court for getting a rule or order to direct some act in favour of applicant. (1) motion to dismiss: It is an application made by defendant to ask the judge dismiss the case; (2) motion for judgment on the pleadings: It is an application made (after pleadings have been entered) to request the court to issue a judgement at that point; (3) motion *in limine*: It is application to ask the court to exclude certain evidence.

18. without prejudice: It means a claim, lawsuit, or proceeding has been brought to a temporary end but that no legal rights have been determined. The parties could continue the further proceedings.

19. with prejudice: It means a party's legal rights have been determined. The term used

in a judgement of dismissal or court decision is as conclusive of the rights of parties.

20. burden of proof: It refers to the responsibility of proving a fact in the trail. In general, the party making a factual allegation has the burden of proof to that allegation. It contains the burden of producing evidence, burden of persuasion, and burden of going forward with the evidence.

21. direct examination: The first interrogation or examination of a witness on the merits of the case by the party on whose behalf the witness is called.

22. cross-examination: The examination of a witness by the adverse party about his evidence to test the truth or further develop it.

23. reverse: The appellate court overturns a lower court's decision.

24. vacate: The court cancels or rescinds the rendered judgment or order.

25. suspend: To stay the enforcement of a judgment or decree.

26. affirm: The appellate court declares the lower court's decision is valid and correct.

27. modify: The appellate court modes or amends the minor defect or insufficiency in the lower court's decision without reversing.

28. remand: The appellate court sends the case back to the lower court for further proceedings with instructions to correct the irregularities.

29. rehearing: A second hearing by the same court to reconsider the decision made after the first hearing.

30. decree: It is the part of the appellate court's decision that issued the conclusion of an action and disposition of the entire case.

B. Common Legal Terms in Criminal Litigation

1. prosecution: It is a criminal action charged and tried by the government attorney against a person accused of a crime.

2. warrant: It is a written order from a judicial officer to authorize the arrest of an individual or the search of property.

3. initial appearance: It refers to a court proceeding when (1) the accused is told of the charges; (2) a decision on bail is made, and (3) arrangements for the next judicial proceeding are specified.

4. felony: It refers to the serious crime to be punishable by the sentence of one year or more.

5. assigned counsel: The private lawyer appointed by the state to provide representation for indigent persons to handle particular cases.

6. pro bono counsel: It refers to the attorney who provide free legal services. In the United States, licensed attorneys are generally required to provide pro bono services for indigent persons for certain hours.

7. bail: (1) As a noun, it refers to the money or bond put up to secure the release of a person charged with a crime. (2) As a verb, it means posting money or bond to secure an accused defendant's release.

8. bond: A written obligation to pay to the court the amount of money specified in the court order fixing bail, executed by the defendant or one or more sureties, in order to insure that the defendant will reappear in court at designated time.

9. personal recognizance: A kind of bail for pre-trial release based on the defendant's own promise that he will appear for trial at designated time. It is used in place that no bail money is required.

10. probable cause: It means having more evidence for conviction than against the criminal charges complained of.

11. grand jury: In the United States, a grand jury is a prosecuting body that presides over on a daily basis by a prosecutor. A grand jury serves for a term of one year and is usually selected from a list of nominees offered by the court in the county or federal district. It investigates crimes by its subpoena power to determine if a prosecution is justified.

12. plead: It means to deliver a formal manner the defendant's answer to the prosecution's or plaintiff's declaration, complaint or indictment. In a criminal case, to plead means to admit or deny the charges as made by the prosecutor.

13. plea (*n.*): It means a formal answer made by a defendant in response to the plaintiff's or prosecution's declaration.

14. plea bargain: It refers to a negotiation process between the accused and the prosecutor to reach a mutual disposition of the case subject to court approval. It usually involves the defendant's pleading guilty to a lesser offense in return for a lighter sentence or the prosecution's dropping some graver charges. Sometimes plea bargain is used to encourage the defendant to reveals other criminal partners.

15. indictment: It is a formal written accusation from a prosecutor, found and issued by a grand jury, against a party charged with a felony. An indictment must be proved at trial beyond a reasonable doubt before the defendant may be convicted.

16. arraignment: After the grand jury proceeding, it is the initial appearance of a criminal defendant before the court.

17. voir dire: It is the preliminary examination that the court may use to test the suitability of a juror or witness. All jurors will be asked to speak the truth when questioned. A juror may be objected out of the jury according to the competency interest, bias, availability, and etc.

18. sentence: It forms the final act of the judgment process. The sentence generally involves a decree of imprisonment and punishment against the convicted defendant.

19. impeach: To discredit a witness by adducing his evidence or by adducing of proof that a witness is unworthy of belief.

20. acquit: To legally and formally certify the innocence of a person charged with crime. (1) Acquittals in fact means that the jury finds a verdict of not guilty; (2) Acquittals in law means a mere operation of law.

C. Common Abbreviated Terms in Case Reading

Abbreviations Related to Arbitral Reports.

Abbreviation—Full Form

1. Arb. Mat'l—Arbitration Materials

2. Hague Ct. Rep. (Scott)—Hague Court Reports, First Series

3. Hague Ct. Rep. 2d (Scott)—Hague Court Reports, Second Series

4. ICSID (W. Bank)—International Center for Settlement of Investment Disputes (World Bank ICSID)

5. Int'l Comm. Arb.—International Chamber of Commerce Arbitration

6. Iran-U.S. Cl. Trib. Rep.—Iran-United States Claims Tribunal Reports

7. R.I.A.A.—United Nations Reports of International Arbitral Awards

8. World Arb. Rep.—World Arbitration Reporter

Abbreviations related to court names

Abbreviation—Full Form

1. Adm.—Admiralty

2. App. Div.—Supreme Court, Appellate Division (State of New York)

3. Admin—Administrative

4. App.—Appeals/Appellate

5. B.T.A.—Board of Tax Appeals

6. Bankr.—Bankruptcy

7. B.I.A.—Board of Immigration Appeals

8. B.P.A.I.—— Patent Appeals & Interferences

9. C.A.—Court of Appeals

10. Ct. App.—Court of Appeals
11. C.C.—Circuit Court
12. Cir. Ct. App.—Circuit Court of Appeals (State)
13. Crim. App.—Court of Criminal Appeals
14. Civ. App.—Civil Appeals
15. Comm'n—Commission
16. Concil.—Conciliation
17. C.D.—Central District
18. Dist. Ct.—District Court
19. Div.—Division
20. Sup. Ct.—Supreme Court

Abbreviations related to court documents

Abbreviation—Full Form

1. Admis.—Admission
2. Am.—Amended
3. Ans.—Answer
4. Attach.—Attachment
5. Aff.—Affidavit
6. Att'y[s]—Attorney[s]
7. Br.—Brief
8. Compl.—Complaint
9. Ct.—Court
10. Decl.—Declaration
11. Defs.[']—Defendants['][.]
12. Disc.—Discovery
13. Hr'g—Hearing
14. Mem.—Memorandum
15. Mot.—Motion
16. Pl.'s—Plaintiff's
17. Rep.—Reporter
18. Summ.—Summary
19. Test.—Testimony
20. V.S.—Verified Statement

Abbreviations related to explanatory phrases

Abbreviation—Full Form

1. Acq.—Acquiescence
2. Acq. in result—Acquiescence in result
3. Aff'd—Affirmed
4. Aff'd on reh'g—Affirmed on rehearing
5. Aff'g—Affirming
6. Cert. denied—Certiorari denied
7. Cert. dismissed—Certiorari dismissed
8. Cert. granted—Certiorari granted
9. Nonacq.—Non-acquiescence
10. Rev'd—Reversed
11. Rev'g—Reversing

Section 3　Common Terms in Contract Drafting

For the convenience of the readers and writers, this section provides the common terms and phrases in contract drafting.

A. Agreement and Contract

agency agreement

bilateral agreement

bilateral trade agreement

commercial agreement

compensation trade agreement

distributorship agreement

exclusive distributorship agreement

guarantee agreement

joint venture agreement

licensing agreement

management agreement

multilateral trade agreement

trade agreement

agency contract

Appendix Legal Vocabulary

ad referendum contract

binding contract

blank form contract

commercial contract

compensation trade contract

cross licence contract

exclusive licence contract

firm sale contract

formal contract

forward contract

import contract

indirect contract

installment contract

international trade contract

long-term contract

non-transferable licence contract

patent licence contract

prime contract

provisional contract

purchase contract

sales contract

sole licence contract

trade mark licence contract

contract for service

contract of affreightment

contract of carriage

contract of carriage by sea

contract of future delivery

contract of guaranty

cancellation of contract

execute of contract

interpretation of contract

performance of contract

termination of contract

fulfil a contract

implement a contract

keep a contract

make a contract with

B. Price

actual price

agreement price

average price

average unit price

basic price

buying price

cash price

closing price

contract price

cost price

delivery price

firm price

fixed price

forward price

free delivery price

invoice price

landed price

mill net price

net selling price

C. Payment

advance payment

at once payment

cash payment

due payment

easy payment

exchange payment

installment payment

transfer payment

payment against arrival

payment against arrival of documents

payment against documents

payment against documents through collection

payment against presentation of shipping documents

payment at sight

payment by bill

payment by cash

payment by check

payment by draft

payment by installments

payment on delivery

payment on demand

payment upon the arrival of shipping documents

payable by installment

payable on the installment

payable at a definite time

payable at a fixed date

payable at usance

D. Certificate

acceptance certificate

delivery and acceptance certificate

exchange surrender certificate

insurance certificate

manufacturer's certificate

mill's certificate

paying certificate

plant quarantine certificate

shipping company's certificate

work's inspection certificate

certificate of acceptance

certificate of competency

certificate of damage

certificate of delivery

certificate of import licence

certificate of incorporation

certificate of independent public surveyor

certificate of inspection

certificate of loss or damage

certificate of loss or damage by carrier

certificate of manufacture

certificate of origin

certificate of quality

certificate of quantity

certificate of quality test

certificate of receipt

certificate of shipment

certificate of soundness

certificate of superintendent

certificate of tare weight

certificate of weight

certificate of weight and measurements

inspection certificate of origin

inspection certificate of quality

inspection certificate of quantity

certificate on hold/tank

certificate on cargo weight and measurements

E. Letter of Credit

assignable credit

bank credit

clean credit

documentary credit

irrevocable credit

negotiation credit

payment on receipt credit

reimbursement credit
revocable credit
revolving credit
stand-by credit
transmissible credit
ancillary letter of credit
clean letter of credit
commercial letter of credit
commercial documentary letter of credit
documentary letter of credit
export letter of credit
guaranteed letter of credit
import letter of credit
open letter of credit
original letter of credit
unassignable letter of credit

F. Document

ancillary document
basic document
claims document
combined on documents
copy document
original document
shipping document
transport document
underlying document
written document
document for claims
document for carriage
document of shipping
documents against payment
documents against payment after date
documents against payment at sight

G. Invoice

commercial invoice

consular invoice

cost and freight invoice

custom's invoice

duplicate invoice

final invoice

official invoice

proforma invoice

provisional invoice

sales invoice

shipping invoice

supplier's invoice

invoice amount

invoice duplicate

invoice for sales

invoice price

invoice value

H. Bill of Lading

airway bill

clean bill of lading

collection bill of lading

consignment bill of lading

dirty bill of lading

export bill of lading

import bill of lading

bill of goods

bill of freight

bill of health

bill of lading

bill of lading to order

bill of particulars

bill of payment

on board bill of lading

order bill of lading

I. Delivery

actual delivery

cash against delivery

cash on delivery

collect on delivery

contractual delivery

forward delivery

near delivery

partial delivery

payment on delivery

prompt delivery

delivery advice

place of delivery

port of delivery

time of delivery

J. Risk and Insurance

abnormal risk

accessory risk

air risk

all risks

customary risk

desk risk

extraneous risk

fire risk

loading and unloading risk

marine risk

total risk

transportation risk

risk of non-delivery

risk of warehouse to warehouse

actual total loss

compromised total loss technical total loss
accident insurance
additional insurance
burglary insurance
cargo insurance
cargo marine insurance
cargo transportation insurance
carrier's liability insurance
collision insurance
comprehensive insurance
concurrent insurance
direct insurance
fire insurance
freight insurance
full insurance
full value insurance
land transit insurance
marine cargo insurance
certificate of insurance
duration of insurance
policy of insurance
premium on insurance
prepaid insurance
guarantee of insurance policy
insurance certificate
sum insured
insured amount
to insure the goods the buyer's account
to arrange (an) insurance on ...
to cover insurance on ....
to effect out insurance on ....
to provide insurance on ...
to take out insurance on ....

References

一、中文著作类

1. 胡耕申. 怎样起草与翻译合同协议 [M]. 北京：中国科技大学出版社，1993.
2. 陈庆柏. 涉外经济法律英语（第三版）[M]. 北京：法律出版社，2007.
3. 孙万彪. 英汉法律翻译教程 [M]. 上海：上海外语教育出版社，2003.
4. 陶博. 法律英语：中英双语法律文书制作 [M]. 上海：复旦大学出版社，2004.
5. 何主宇. 涉外法律函电英文写作范例 [M]. 北京：法律出版社，2005.
6. 吕立山，江宪胜. 合同与法律咨询文书制作技能 [M]. 北京：法律出版社，2007.
7. 董世忠，赵建. 法律英语 [M]. 上海：复旦大学出版社，2007.
8. 王辉. 英文合同解读 [M]. 北京：法律出版社，2007.
9. 杨俊峰. 法律英语案例探究 [M]. 北京：清华大学出版社，2007.
10. 金岳霖. 逻辑 [M]. 北京：中国人民大学出版社，2010.
11. 李克兴. 英汉法律翻译案例讲评 [M]. 北京：外文出版社，2011.
12. 纳迪尔·E. 内奇尔. 法律推理、研究与写作方法 [M]. 王润贵，王林，译，北京：知识产权出版社，2013.
13. 王相国. 鏖战英文合同：英文合同的翻译与起草（第三版）[M]. 北京：中国法制出版社，2018.
14. 高玉美，王刚. 涉外法律文书范本 [M]. 北京：世界知识出版社，2015.
15. 屈文生，石伟. 法律英语阅读与翻译教程（第三版）[M]. 上海：上海人民出版社，2023.
16. 张法连. 法律英语写作教程 [M]. 北京：北京大学出版社，2016.
17. 费尔迪南·德·索绪尔. 普通语言学教程 [M]. 高名凯，译. 北京：商务印书馆，2017.

18. 张振林，姜芳. 法律英语术语说文解字[M]. 北京：中国政法大学出版社，2019.

二、外文论著类

1. Walker & David M. *The Oxford Companion to Law (1st Edition)*[M]. Oxford: Clarendon Press Oxford University Press, 1980.

2. Jay Folberg & Alison Taylor. *Mediation: A Comprehensive Guide to Resolving Conflicts Without Litigation (1st Edition)*[M]. San Francisco: JosseyBass, 1984.

3. Laurence Boulle & Miryana Nesic. *Mediation: Principles, Process, Practice (1st Edition)*[M]. London: Butterworths, 2001.

4. Xuebo. *English-Chinese Dictionary of Anglo-American Law (1st Edition)*[M]. Beijing: Law Press China, 2003.

5. Peter Butt & Richard Castle. *Modern Legal Drafting: A Guide to Using Clearer Language (2nd Edition)*[M]. Cambridge: Cambridge University Press, 2006.

6. Paul Richards & Leslie B. Curzon. *The Longman Dictionary of Law (7th Edition)*[M]. Harlow: Pearson Education Limited, 2007.

7. Linda S. Abrams & Kevin P. McGuinness. *Canadian Civil Procedure Law*[M]. Markham: LexisNexis, 2008.

8. Frederick Schauer. *Thinking Like a Lawyer: A New Introduction to Legal Reasoning*[M]. Cambridge, MA: Harvard University Press, 2009.

9. John P. H. Soper. *A Treatise on the Law and Practice of Arbitrations and Awards: For Surveyors, Valuers, Auctioneers and Estate Agents*[M]. London: London Estates Gazette, 2010.

10. John C. Dernbarch et al. *A Practice Guide to Legal Writing and Legal Method*[M]. Alphen aan den Rijn: Wolters Kluwer, 2010.

11. Steven D. Stark. *Writing to Win: The Legal Writer*[M]. New York: Three River Press, 2012.

12. Bryan A. Garner. *Legal Writing in Plain English: A Text with Exercises*[M]. Chicago: The University of Chicago Press, 2013.

13. James Hooland et al. *Learning Legal Rules*[M]. Oxford: Oxford University Press, 2013.

14. Carol M. Bast. *Legal Research and Writing*[M]. Clifton Park: Delmar Cengage Learning, 2013.

15. Lisa Webley. *Legal Writing*[M]. Abingdon: Routledge, 2013.

16. Hope Viner Samborn, Andrea B. *Basic Legal Writing for Paralegals*[M]. Alphen aan den Rijn: Wolters Kluwer, 2013.

17. Mary Barnard Ray, Barbara J. Cox. Beyond the Basics: *A Text for Advanced Legal Writing*[M]. Durham: Carolina Academic Press, 2013.

18. Christopher Moore. *The Mediation Process: Practical Strategies for Resolving Conflict (4th Edition)*[M]. San Francisco: JosseyBass, 2014.

19. Amy Krois-Lindner et al. *International Legal English*[M]. Cambridge: Cambridge University Press, 2014.

20. Jacqueline Martin. *English Legal System*[M]. Abingdon: Routledge, 2014.

21. Stephen Breyer. *The Court and the World: American Law and the New Global Realities*[M]. New York: Alfred A. Knopf, 2015.

22. William Searle Holdsworth. *A History of English Law*[M]. Andesite Press, 2015.

23. Phil Harris. *An Introduction to Law*[M]. Cambridge: Cambridge University Press, 2016.

24. Allan Ides, Christopher N. May & Simona Grossi. *Civil Procedure: Constitution, Statutes, Rules and Supplemental Materials*[M]. Alphen aan den Rijn: Wolters Kluwer, 2017.

25. Joseph W. Glannon, Andrew M. Perlman, Peter Raven-Hansen. *Civil Procedure: A Coursebook*[M]. Alphen aan den Rijn: Wolters Kluwer, 2017.

26. Bryan A. Garner. *Black's Law Dictionary (11th Edition)*[M]. St. Paul: Thomson Reuters West, 2019.

27. Trevor C. Hartley. *International Commercial Litigation: Text, Cases and Materials on Private International Law (3rd Edition.)*[M]. Cambridge: Cambridge University Press, 2020.

三、外文论文类

1. Sturges, W. A. Arbitration—What is it[J]. *New York University Law Review*, Vol.35, No.1, 1960. ISSN 0028-7364.

2. Douglas Yarn. The Death of ADR: A Cautionary Tale of Isomorphism Through Institutionalization[J]. *Penn State Law Review*, Vol.108, No.3, 2004. ISSN 0093-8721.

3. Eidenmuller H. & Varesis F. What Is an Arbitration? Artificial Intelligence and the

Vanishing Human Arbitrator[J]. *New York University Journal of Law and Business*, Vol.16, No.3, 2020. ISSN 1540-8838.

四、外文网站类

1. AAA, *About Us*, at https://www.adr.org/mission.

2. AAA, *Commercial Arbitration Rules and Mediation Procedures*, at https://www.adr.org/sites/default/files/Commercial-Rules-Web.pdf.

3. Arbitration lawyer, *European Convention on International Commercial Arbitration*, at http://www.arbitrationlawyer.cn/html/1375.html.

4. CCPIT, *Mediation Center*, at https://adr.ccpit.org.

5. CIETAC, *About Us*, at http://www.cietac.org/index.php?m=Page&a=index&id=34&l=en.

6. CIETAC, *Model Arbitration Clause*, at http://www.cietac.org/index.php?m=Article&a=show&id=216.

7. HKIAC, *About Us*, https://www.hkiac.org/about-us.

8. HKIAC, *Model Clauses*, at https://www.hkiac.org/arbitration/modelclauses#Domestic%20Arbitration%20under%20the%20HKIAC%20Domestic%20Arbitration%20Rules.

9. HKIAC, *Hong Kong International Arbitration Centre Mediation Rules*, at https://www.hkiac.org/mediation/rules/hkiac-mediation-rules.

10. ICC, *About Us*, at https://iccwbo.org/about-us/who-we-are/.

11. ICC, *2021 Arbitration Rules*, at https://iccwbo.org/content/uploads/sites/3/2020/12/icc-2021-arbitration-rules-2014-mediation-rules-english-version.pdf.

12. LCIA, *About Us*, at https://lcia.org/LCIA/organisation.aspx.

13. LCIA, *Recommended Clauses*, at https://www.lcia.org/Dispute_Resolution_Services/LCIA_Mediation_Clauses.aspx.

14. OAS, *Inter-American Convention on International Commercial Arbitration*, at http://www.oas.org/en/sla/dil/inter_american_treaties_B-35_international_commercial_arbitration.asp.

15. OAS, *Inter-American Convention on Extraterritorial Validity of Foreign Judgments and Arbitral Awards*, at http://www.oas.org/juridico/english/treaties/b-41.html.

16. OAS, *International Commercial Arbitration*, at http://www.oas.org/en/sla/dil/docs/

International_Commercial_Arbitration_BROCHURE_En.pdf.

17. Queen Marry University of London, *2010 International Arbitration Survey: Choices in International Arbitration*, at http://www.arbitration.qmul.ac.uk/media/arbitration/docs/2010_InternationalArbitrationSurveyReport.pdf.

18. SCC, *About Us*, at https://sccinstitute.com/about-the-scc/.

19. SCC, *2017 Arbitration Rules*, at https://sccinstitute.com/media/1407444/arbitration rules_eng_2020.pdf.

20. SCC, *Model Clauses*, at https://sccinstitute.com/our-services/model-clauses/.

21. UNCITRAL, *Convention on the Recognition and Enforcement of Foreign Arbitral Awards*, at https://uncitral.un.org/sites/uncitral.un.org/files/media-documents/uncitral/en/new-york-convention-e.pdf.SIAC, *About us*, at https://siac.org.sg/.

22. SIAC, *Arbitration Rules of the Singapore International Arbitration Centre (2016)*, at https://www.siac.org.sg/images/stories/articles/rules/2016/SIAC%20Rules%202016%20English_28%20Feb%2020 17.pdf.

23. SIMC, *Mediation Rules*, at https://simc.com.sg/v2/wp-content/uploads/2020/10/SIMCMediationRules-EN-FINAL_A4-updated-16-Oct-2020.pdf.

24. UNCITRAL, *UNCITRAL Model Law on International Commercial Arbitration*, at https://uncitral.un.org/sites/uncitral.un.org/files/media-documents/uncitral/en/19-09955_e_ebook.pdf.

25. UNCITRAL, *UNCITRAL Secretariat Guide on the Convention on the Recognition and Enforcement of Foreign Arbitral Awards*, at https://uncitral.un.org/sites/uncitral.un.org/files/mediadocuments/uncitral/en/2016_guide_on_the_convention.pdf.

26. UNCITRAL, *United Nations Convention on International Settlement Agreements Resulting from Mediation*, at https://uncitral.un.org/en/texts/mediation/conventions/international_settlement_agreements/.

27. UNECE, *Revision of the 1961 European Convention on International Commercial Arbitration*, at https://unece.org/fileadmin/DAM/trade/ctied5/trade0116e.pdf.

28. WIPO, *Alternative Dispute Resolution*, at https://www.wipo.int/amc/en/.

29. WIPO, *Guide to WIPO Mediation*, at https://www.wipo.int/edocs/pubdocs/en/wipo_pub_449_2018.pdf.

图书在版编目(CIP)数据

法律文书写作与推理：英文 / 张正怡等编著.
上海：上海社会科学院出版社，2025. -- ISBN 978-7
-5520-4618-2

Ⅰ.D916.13
中国国家版本馆 CIP 数据核字第 20245L9X09 号

法律文书写作与推理

编　　著：	张正怡　钱沂青　黄珮琦　范瑞娟　秦　朗
责任编辑：	董汉玲
封面设计：	裘幼华
出版发行：	上海社会科学院出版社
	上海顺昌路 622 号　邮编 200025
	电话总机 021－63315947　销售热线 021－53063735
	https://cbs.sass.org.cn　E-mail：sassp@sassp.cn
照　　排：	南京理工出版信息技术有限公司
印　　刷：	上海颛辉印刷厂有限公司
开　　本：	710 毫米×1010 毫米　1/16
印　　张：	14.25
插　　页：	2
字　　数：	365 千
版　　次：	2025 年 1 月第 1 版　2025 年 1 月第 1 次印刷

ISBN 978－7－5520－4618－2/D·744　　　　　　　　　　定价：88.00 元

版权所有　翻印必究